Lewis W. Hine

*"Hine was one of the Greats. I don't know a
photographer who has not been conscious of, and
influenced to some extent by, Lewis Hine."*

Ben Shahn

WALKER AND COMPANY • NEW YORK

LEWIS W. HINE

and the American social conscience

JUDITH MARA GUTMAN

ACKNOWLEDGEMENTS

The author would like to acknowledge her debt to those who very kindly
gave her permission to reproduce the following photographs:

On pages 61, 63, 66-7, 102, 108, 110-11, 113-14,
116-17, 121, 131, 133-35, 137-40, 142-45,
courtesy of George Eastman House; on pages
64, 107, 109, 112, courtesy of Ewing Galloway;
on pages 62, 106, 119-20, courtesy of the
American History Division, The New York
Public Library, Astor, Lenox and Tilden
Foundations; on pages 65, 68-101, 103-5, 115,
118, courtesy of the National Child Labor
Committee; on pages 122-30, 132, 136, 146,
150, 156, courtesy of the Library of Congress;
on page 141, courtesy Avery Library, Columbia
University; on page 149, courtesy of the
Picture Collection, The New York Public
Library; on pages 147-48, 151-54, courtesy of
Tennessee Valley Authority; on page 155,
courtesy of the American Red Cross.

Book designed by Lena Fong Lueg

Library of Congress Catalog Card Number:
LC 67-23089

First published in the United States of America
in 1967 by Walker and Company, a division of
Walker Publishing Company, Inc.

Published simultaneously in Canada by
The Ryerson Press, Toronto

Printed in the United States of America

Contents

Preface

TWO HUNDRED AND SEVEN PEOPLE helped write this book. Each of the two hundred and seven scratched open surfaces—present and past—to look, suggest, come up with, and meander with letters, photographs, thoughts, meetings, conferences, chance occurrences, memories of — particular facets in which Lewis Wickes Hine figured. Some searched in libraries, some in their thoughts. Others called on relatives; some never knew, heard of, or could respond to Hine — but put me in touch with someone who did or might have. Each did a different thing and like a pyramid revealing rugged and different facets as it begins to rise above a landscape, the two hundred and seven people brought unique factors to my attention, and the book reflects them.

The book started off as a re-discovery of a man and his work—a creditable enough venture. But it grew into an outright discovery, in large measure because of these clusters of thoughts and people. They found, or, as often happened, enabled me to find, photographs which had never before been seen, identified, or published. About fifty per cent of the photographs in this book have never before been published. That panorama created a huge new question: why? Why was a particular part of Hine available and another by-passed? For whom did Hine create? Knowingly? For which age? Consciously? How much of an artist was he? How much of a reformer? How did he make each facet function? What created the discrepancy? Hine's

jarring, out-of-focus, relationship with a century that initially bore him, together with his absolute involvement in his own early period, helped create the cornerstones—for the search and the book. That the by-passed was relevant and beautiful only made the questions more intriguing.

The book started—perhaps it is more precise to think of it germinating—at the George Eastman House, where Mr. Beaumont Newhall, Director of the Gallery-Library, opened all of the Hine material he had acquired to me, his own as well as the library's. It was he, of course, in the 1950's, who accepted the notes, glass and film negatives, letters, scraps, and photographic prints that the Photo League had acquired from Hine at the time of his death, accepted that collection when no other gallery in and out of New York spoke for it. It was also he who found Hine back in 1938 living halfway between poverty and reality. Once I was exposed to the various patterns and images Hine created and saw both the intensity and the suavity, the directness and the indirectness, a book on Hine seemed necessary: one can never put away a haunting idea. The people at George Eastman House were most helpful. But Mr. Newhall must be singled out; and it is fitting that it was from the institution he heads that a book on Hine should get off the ground.

Once it did, the book expanded. Ideas, suggestions, and resources poured in and provided quickly multiplying routes for the book to take. Mr. Ned Chase, editor at New American Library, suggested I see Miss Louise Kapp of the National Committee on the Employment for Youth—see her, he suggested, and look at the photographs she keeps in the file she operates for that organization. The photographs were all Hine photographs—five thousand that he did for the old National Child Labor Committee, of which about five hundred—at best—had ever been published. She talked about the people she had heard of and/or knew who knew Hine, suggested I visit with some, allowed me to borrow the Hine photographs I would need, and introduced me to Mr. Eli E. Cohen, the Executive Secretary of the NCEY, who permitted the reproduction of Hine's NCLC photographs for this book.

Living with five thousand Hine photographs, most of them taken within an eight year period of time, seeing the three and five and seven printings he would sometimes make of one exposure, and watching the flow of chronologically ordered photographs brought me close to the order Hine created as he moved from boy to scene to factory to town. I saw which he favored, how rarely he ever changed a negative, and saw, for instance, how far his mind must have been from the whole discussion of gum prints raging at the same time. I saw how committed he was and first suspected how alone he was. When Miss Kapp suggested I see Gertrude Folks Zimand, then still alive but terribly sick, I waited . . . and never saw her. After she died, I did see her husband, Mr. Savel Zimand, talked and chatted with him, found out that he knew Hine quite independent of his wife—"but not as well", he added—and started moving along one of those circles that the search for this book was to create again and again.

When the National Child Labor Committee changed its focus and name in 1954, it gave its early scrapbooks—manuscripts and photographs—to the Library of Congress. In the Library of Congress, in both the Manuscript division and the Prints and Photographs division, I met only the most cooperative, gracious and untiring help. Each person I met—from the head of a division on down: Mr. Edgar Breitenbach, Mr. Alan Fern, Miss Virginia Daiker, Mr. LeRoy Bellamy—each extended his role so completely that I was able finally to locate and identify approximately one thousand Hine photographs in the uncatalogued American Red Cross Collection. Mr. David C. Mearns, chief of the Manuscript division, suggested other possible manuscript sources; and when the question of reproduction was discussed, Mr. Donald C. Holmes of the Photoduplication Service personally discussed and oversaw the quality of his staff's work to assure quality reproductions.

At the National Archives, I found photographs of his WPA work. Mr. Hill and Mr. Maxwell located some telegrams for me; but although WPA correspondence from Hine is available from Hine sources, government-held records could not be located.

The circle of help continued when I visited the

American Red Cross in Washington, D.C. Miss Kidwell, Librarian of the American Red Cross, searched out their archives, came up with old records, introduced me to Mr. Rudy Vetter and Mr. Cliff Valentine of the Photographic staff; and between them all, allowed me entry into their files where once again we were able to discover lost Hine photographs, many of them from the '20's and '30's, showing in effect the jobs he held.

Living within an unexplored Hine world, and coming continually upon never-before-lifted layers of his life and work, I was often amazed when something failed to materialize. I never found out enough about the Hine Photo Company. I suspect Paul Schumm worked for Hine. Paul Parker may have. A part of the story breaks off....

...but then picks up suddenly again when I located the complete correspondence that Lewis Hine had with Paul Kellogg from 1918 to 1940—all during which time Paul Kellogg was editor of *Survey* magazine. Kellogg was friend as well as editor; and I thank Prof. Clarke Chambers, Director of the Social Welfare History Archives Center at the University of Minnesota and Miss Andrea Hinding, both of whom helped get that file to me, and showed me the fifty Hine prints they have. While I was researching there, the records of the National Recreation Association arrived. Intact, they stood against the stone warehouse wall warming it against the −32° outside, too freshly arrived to be opened. Hine photographs may be in those boxes.

When I went to Knoxville, Tennessee to look at the TVA photos Hine took in late 1933 I met Mr. Gilbert Stewart, Jr., head of TVA's Office of Information, and once again felt moved along a chain of events. He introduced me to Mr. Billy Glenn who runs the Graphics Department and whose first job when he came to TVA in 1934 was to develop the Hine negatives. But he went beyond that and first searching through old government records that were no longer even in Knoxville, was able to locate telegrams and letters involving Hine in the '30's, and then located people who had met Hine when he came into the area.

In New York, Mr. Barry Baragwanath of the Museum of the City of New York showed me the Museum's reprint Hine collection, but also brought me to see a diorama the Museum keeps of the Empire State Building that was modeled on Hine's Empire State photographs. Miss Ramona Javitz of the New York Public Library's Picture Service Collection talked with me of her meetings with Hine in the mid 1930's. Mr. MacDonald of the Local History Room of the New York Public Library suggested people I might meet. Mr. Gil Burck, editor of *Fortune*, told me he wrote his first—probably trial—story for *Fortune* in 1939 on Railroad Firemen; Hine photographed for the same story. Mr. Allister of Brown Brothers talked with me of the thousands of stereos and plates they bought in the century's first decades, many of them bought from stereo companies, many of them probably Hine stereos, many of them probably bought from the Hine Photo Company. But they have no records. And then another whole group of people opened files and records for me.

Mr. Placzek and Miss Stone of Columbia University's Avery Library let me wander through their Empire State Collection. Its photos were dustier than the Red Cross's. Mr. Joseph Hisler of Ewing Galloway searched out their inactive files and came up with over one hundred photos they have. Mrs. Louise Heinze, former librarian of the Tamiment Library, lent me the dozen or so Hines she had. Mrs. Mary Carr Webb, long-time secretary to Al Smith, lent me her personal autographed copy of *Empire State,* a hardback limited-edition book commemorating the opening of the building. Hine photographs illustrate the triumph they all felt. Miss Minna Goosman of the Ethical Culture Society gave me straight biographical information and then found other photographs Hine did in the '30's for the school. Mrs. Mary McGurk of Russell Sage Foundation supplied me with xeroxed copies of their files involving Lewis Hine, most of it from Hine's last years when he was preparing his documentary portfolio.

I spoke with Mr. Richard Kellogg, son of Paul Kellogg, Miss Helen Hall, wife of Paul, Mrs. John Fitch, wife to the John Fitch who had written one of the original *Pittsburgh Survey* volumes and knew Hine in the '20's and '30's, too. I had hoped to find more photographs, some letters, and hopefully, some of the other original prints and negatives from the *Pittsburgh Survey.* Another unfruitful end. When Mrs. Fitch's daughter searched the basement of their upstate New York home and could find nothing more, I decided to stop pursuing that phase.

But the rest of the Empire State collection might be found. Only about four hundred and fifty out of one thousand exposures can be traced between Avery Library and the George Eastman House. When I spoke with Mr. Carlos Israels, son of Belle (Israels) Moscowitz, he tried very hard. No material emerged.

On a cold New Year's Day in New York, I spoke with Mr. Paul Strand, photographer *extraordinaire.* Strand had studied with Hine in 1908 and trying to recapture some of the flavor of Hine's—he called it "courage"—Strand reminded me that when nobody else dared, Hine photographed conflict. Photographing child labor, especially in the South, was akin to entering an armed camp, Strand continued. Although struck by its uniqueness as he spoke, I chose to ignore that fact in writing this book. Hine's brilliance seemed much more necessary a focus: his humanity functioned with, not distinct from, his art. But, recently, as a photographer and journalist were killed in the Israeli-Egyptian War and others slipped by death in the Newark and Detroit riots, my compassion for Hine's choice of route for expressing his sense of humanity has increased. I thank Paul Strand.

Friends always occupy a special and perhaps even

peculiar place. They're helpful without realizing it, and don't realize how helpful they are. Miss Grace Mayer of the Museum of Modern Art in New York City will claim she did nothing . . . and using a standard system of measurements, she might be right: nothing tangible from her exists in this book. But her steadfast excitement and desire for the book continually supported me. Mr. Joseph Kastner of *Life* created a different sort of support. He simply wanted to hear about the book: but producing my thoughts with a characteristically gentle but clear sharp edge, he unwittingly made me re-think flimsily held ideas. Mr. Grant Taplin, an economist with the International Monetary Fund—of all things—dependably researched and checked for me from his Washington berth while I was in California. Professor Albert Hofstadter, now at the University of California at Santa Cruz, then at the Center for Advanced Study in the Behavioral Sciences, engaged himself so thoroughly with aesthetic-realist principles that many of my early aesthetic judgments came out of those early conversations. One friend, Mr. Edward L. Burlingame, became my editor. That has its own particular, and overwhelming, support.

I never met Robert M. Doty, Associate Curator of the Whitney Museum, until this book was well under way. But Mr. Doty was the first of the present generation of people to wake to Hine. He started work some seven or eight years ago when he was at the George Eastman House, but never continued, and when I met him, he offered me his notes. It is easy enough, I guess, to thank him for his notes. But for one so involved in material to offer that material suggests a superior act of graciousness. I thank him first for that, and then for the material.

Mr. Corydon Hine, son of Lewis Hine, responded succinctly and precisely to questions I asked, and when he could not answer, bowed deferentially to those who could.

Marta and Nell, my daughters, put up with my preoccupation: grew callous to, annoyed with, fond of, mildly interested in; and even put in a modest—no, tiny—share of picture search for the bibliography. And Herb? Absolute and husbandly. His enormous range confronted me and the material all the time. Intellectually demanding and personally admiring, he shifted between his professorial world, a home world, and a new twentieth-century Hine world growing up all around us.

Two occupy a distinct place. My mother and father first made me aware of a human being's potential. A portion of this book belongs only to them.

STANFORD, CALIFORNIA
SUMMER 1967

Lewis Hine

IN 1908 LEWIS WICKES HINE PROUDLY announced himself a photographer and filled his first advertisement in *Charities and Commons* with twenty-two close lines of type, each word a tiny shy intrusion on the great new public burgeoning in the new American cities. Within a year or two, he opened a studio, employed a staff, catalogued his work, developed film for a newly conscious film-paying public, and made slides of the photographs he took for the National Child Labor Committee when he addressed its members at conferences in 1909, 1910, and the years following. By 1912 he ran a thick black question mark through the center of his advertisements. Stereopticons? Call at 27 Grant Avenue, Lincoln Park, Yonkers, New York. And by 1913, he prominently displayed a photograph in the center of his advertisement and recomposed the type and changed that photo for each weekly announcement in *Survey* magazine. Born in Oshkosh, Wisconsin in 1874, he came to New York in 1901, moved first to Yonkers and in 1919 to Hastings-on-the-Hudson with his wife and son (and lived there with his sister, too, until 1940 when he died); and moved through the twentieth century's first two decades as if supported by the volcanic public erupting all about him. Angry at civic ills, compassionate towards human personality, and plagued by an artistic insistence, he seemed to thrive on the rumbling expectation the new demonstrative public served. But he was probably relieved that his camera separated him

from that public, and he exploded quietly—some have said eloquently—by himself.

Hine came to the "new" New York soon after industrialism came to cities; and like so many other early twentieth century reformers wanted to order the chaos that the industrial city was creating. In the last decades of the nineteenth century, industries, population, and labor had grown and shifted. Though an article in *Everybody's* claimed one million farmers "emigrated" to the South West in 1907, over one million immigrants entered the country in the same year. "He is a poor American who does not feel the thrill of Ellis Island," read an editorial in *Outlook,* "yet he is also a foolish American who can visit Ellis Island without questioning...the future." Immigrants as immigrants, laborers, and people emerged from diverse backgrounds, from the town, from the fields, even from nineteenth-century city life; all streamed into the modern city. Small town lines conflicted with the new city patterns just as old city patterns clashed with the new. The city became the center of the country's erratic industrial impulses—and the new industrial centers—towns and cities—became in turn wellsprings of hope and cesspools of despair. Growth, conflict, and expectation excited all those who came in contact with them.

Artists and writers could not remain aloof. Edith Wharton who had found an upper-class soul in nineteenth-century New York found a new nobility among

12

the poor of the twentieth century. Robert Henri, George Luks, and William Glackens, born in Cincinnati, Williamsport (Pennsylvania) and Philadelphia created new urban subjects on canvas. Jane Addams and Florence Kelly shaped new industrial communities in Chicago. Jean-Eugene-Auguste Atget exposed the New Man's pre-existential tragedy in Paris. Pablo Picasso leveled people into planes, reconciled emotions with their existence, and explored their realities. Theodore Dreiser revealed the new emotions which drove people on. And Hine hoped to find a new natural order. Unlike Dreiser he expected to find it in concrete slabs and smoking steel stacks. Reared in the environment of a small town, with little industry and with nature all around, Hine came to the city to seek the new natural goodness rather than stay in the country. He wanted and expected to see a new human magnificence, a transformed humanity rise out of the new industrial seedbed.

Hine expected to find a unity of life and labor in the new city. Much as John Ruskin had suggested to the nineteenth-century English conceptualizations of the organic naturalist's life, and much as William James described Professor Davidson's "becoming almost one with resurgent vegetation" in his woodland cabin, Hine followed a symbolically wooded trail and thought to find a plane of fruitful labor at its end. Nature was already a new religion. Now the city had become a new God. The "New Naturalism" paralleled "The

New New York." The city came to represent, indeed, became, the new organic whole. What had remained passive in a rural nature would become active in its urban counterpart. An editorial in 1906 stated, "We are all now workers as well as employers...fellow-citizens of one great people." The new industrial-urban image attracted all the hopes wooded Nature had traditionally provided. As the new naturalism in the new city would, it was believed, create a new human perfection, so Hine hoped and expected that the craftsman would have a greater, not lesser, place in the new industrial society. One of Hine's favorite photographs was a printer he took in 1905.

Mines and miners attracted Hine more than any other workers. "Other workers are just as human," he wrote to Savel Zimand, then editing the special issue on Coal for *Survey Graphic* in 1922, "but so much less wonderful." Joining earth-ridden nature to an urban industrial seedbed they created a singular image, but the whole nature-urban image produced facets Hine photographed: men, women and children at bobbins, gates, and on docks—people he saw working at the tools of the new age. He associated these people with the varying and multiplying parts of the new world, and inadvertently he wove a new and separate reality out of their ties to this new century.

Inadvertently, for even as he hoped he grew angry. As his hopes for the new century grew, so the impact of what he saw and heard affected him more fully.

13

Tenements stank, deaths rose. Diseases increased. John Spargo called his book "The Bitter Cry of the Children" and when it appeared in 1905 that cry seemed to ring through the streets. Where for the nineteenth century the threshold of expectation had been a natural woodland, the new urban-industrial society thrust forward into the twentieth century—and then choked it. A new chaos came with the new reality.

When Hine saw these "un-natural" industrial by-products choking off the "natural" new urban growth, he turned angrily upon the environment surrounding him, traveling 12,000 miles in the United States alone in 1913. However a person—child or adult—found his relationship to the new industrial world, Hine photographed it. Sweeping. Baking. Waiting. Shipping. House-working. Carrying. Arriving. Existing. Hine concentrated on the relationship that bound a person to his society. In 1924 he was to write of photographing "the common man"—the "you and I" he explained. He caught the harsh reality in scene after scene, face after face, drifting toward children, concerned that they carried "industrial mortgages" on their backs rather than the new urban hope. But he always gravitated toward the individual whether it was a woman, child, or man from the "white collar and underwear stuff." He moved towards an individual and framed him in his setting. Consistently he found that person's strength. Not romanticized strength. Not dramatic power. Just plain insistent human will—the facet that expected so

much from the new age.

In 1905, the same year that Joseph Stella sketched immigrants arriving on Ellis Island, Hine photographed them. In 1907 he photographed slums and Negroes in Washington. In 1908 he started photographing children at play and in the streets. In 1918-19 he explored war-time effects on both people and land in Europe, returning to the United States in 1919. In the 20's he focused primarily on men at their machines. As a climax to the decade and unconsciously as an epitome of his own expectations for the urban industrial century in 1930, he photographed men as they built the Empire State Building. And in 1933, when we see the photographs he recorded for the Tennessee Valley Authority of Clinch Valley, since inundated by Norris Dam waters, we know that he had found a certain respite back amidst the natural setting from which he came. His search for reality had lead him full circle. In the 30's his best photographs are set in rural and small-town America.

That the pattern suggests a statuesque Hine is imperfect—but half true. Hine stayed too completely within his private world of conceptions, his private world of feelings, even his private approach to public things like reform and the young and growing field of photography to stand boldly against the towering background which was emerging. He liked and wanted acclaim. A wan smile must have crept along his face as he read from a friend's letter to him in 1932, "They won't be able to get along without you, no matter what happens. No matter how technocratical we may become, cameras will never be invented that can make more artistic photographs. The more mechanical inventions, the more will skilled artisans be needed to operate them." He wrote to Paul Kellogg in April of 1924, "The Jury for the Art Director's Club Exhibition of Advertising Art . . . gave me *the* medal for *photographs.*" Requests from an ever-increasing number of magazines in 1930-31 made him write in another letter to Paul Kellogg in October of 1930, *"American* magazine is doing a story about my industrial portraiture, old stand-by's,—as 'old friends' that have stood the test of time . . . Their roto-features are always exclusive stuff but they waived that point . . . Voila!" He had earlier instructed students how to compose and use light and in the 30's asked "to see what kind of prints" the TVA was sending out. He thought of himself as an artist and wanted what would have brought him out into the great towering structures the public built.

But as many ties as Hine had with the many publics, and as much as he increased those ties he isolated himself. Self-defined, he multiplied those ties privately amidst the great multiplying public—so privately that by the last decade of his own life when one saw him stooped as usual behind his graflex he "seemed a rather unlikely person to do an assignment of any kind," recalls Seville Osborn of *Fortune.* Thirty years after the Empire State Building went up, an official of that corporation can remember "nothing" of him, and discounts that he was the "official" photographer. Imogen Cunningham, a photographer from San Francisco, visited New York in 1934 and never even knew he was still alive although she would have loved to meet and talk with him. Robert L. Duffus, Editorial Page Editor of the *New York Times* when he resigned after a thirty-six year stay with the *Times* in 1964, and author of *The Valley and Its People, A Portrait of TVA* (Knopf, 1944), never even recognized his name although he used Hine's photographs to illustrate his book.

By the mid-30's, when he lunched—fairly often—with Victor Weybright, then managing editor of *Survey Graphic,* he shrugged off and laughed "drolly," Weybright recalls, at his relatively unknown end-of-life place and poverty. Recommendations consistently referred to his "artistic temperament." "IS TRUE ARTIST TYPE" reads a telegram recommending him to the Rural Electrification Administration in 1935. "REQUIRES HANDLING AS SUCH." And by the end of the decade (his life too) he needed money—desperately. Though generally by-passed, he still hoped that somehow "the results will justify all the bloodshed." But he could never really tell. His desire to perfect an almost pure—not artistically pure, but "Hine-o-graphically" pure—statement engulfed him. Poverty probably never unnerved him until it became intrusive. He could never see himself in a world of people. He saw them. And he felt his own purpose. Meanwhile, outside his perception in the rebalancing moving world he could never fully see the people he photographed appeared more and more statuesque.

And now his photographs seem great. His perceptions turn out to be incisive. From his private world he entered the world of historical realities and captured conflict after conflict, each with humans intricately wound into the reality. Hine never tried hard for a single effect; he was usually not pictorially dramatic and many of his photographs appeared flat — not "shocking enough" to his contemporaries. But his committed eye saw a reality and his camera framed it; and Victor Weybright, who edited Hine material for *Survey Graphic* in the 30's calls Hine's work "photographs of revelation."

And they do reveal a past. But the photographs do not satiate us with their tangible realities. Even though we can no longer see the post against which John Dempsey stood, the floor across which Freddie Reed walked, and the bobbins Leo's hands worked we do not turn to the photographs mainly to find these realities. They're not alive. The people are. The people in the photographs communicate directly to us as if they were still alive. They spill out of their historic reality to become part of our present. We see them and think we are about to know them—see them move, think, or act, as if by approaching them physically we might know more of what made them live spiritually. They make us want to get closer in to them.

Jorge Luis Borges, the Argentinian novelist and essayist, talks of this "imminence of revelation" in great art and as we pass from photograph to photograph we hang on a precipice. We expect that each photograph will reveal more of its life, more of its subject, more of its rhythm and force and counterpoint. Though each photograph reveals an historic completed past, we wait, expecting more.

That gap. That interminably intangible gap that suggests more than it reveals: that grips us. What the eyes seem about to tell us, not what we already know, confronts us. What the people seem ready to spill out of their lives, not what is resolved and contained, meets us. These people exist today; and that existence overshadows their revelation of the past. Though they "document" the past, they live in the present. And though they grew out of an historic reality, they produce an aesthetic reality. They have become timeless and universal and produce infinite realities that exist beyond particular moments in time.

An inauspicious beginning. He came from Oshkosh, Wisconsin, worked in a furniture factory, fooled around with art forms—mainly wood sculpture, went to Oshkosh Normal, then to the University of Chicago where he probably met Dewey and Veblen, went on to New York where he studied further and taught at elementary and high school. He was a local boy in the best sense of the term. He even wrote home to the *Oshkosh Northwestern* in October of 1903 of the environment surrounding New York. The Catskills were spectacular: "I spent the night above the clouds and awoke in the morning to an experience new to me. It was a clear, sunny day, with bright, blue sky overhead. Below, shutting off entirely the view of the lower country, was a mass of white cumulous clouds stretching away to the horizon and looking like a great tempestuous sea with white billows dashing high against the coast, which was in reality made up of the peaks of distant mountains." Even Rip Van Winkle appeared...or almost for "at any crackling of the bushes one turns, half expecting to see the old, bent form with his white hair, tangled beard, and rusty firelock."

Writing of Rip Van Winkle was neither innocent nor accidental. Nature attracted thoughts and energies all across the country. John Muir had convinced a nation to put aside further lands for conservation. Yosemite added state and national acreage. The Shade Tree Commissioners in Newark, New Jersey heard a report that spraying trees effectively saved whole communities of trees. And in Riverside, California, 350 trees were planted in 1904 on the city streets and 2,170 in 1908. Further, one could read of white-tipped elk in the Northwest forest or learn to track the flight of birds; and if one lived and worked in the new city, walk under the gregarious elms that reached out, for example, over Madison Square in New York City.

They spread contentment. A decade later, fundamental plans for garden living in the city would occupy minds and monies, but at the very turn of the century Nature in a pure state occupied a God-like place. When Hine went to the Catskills he extended his woodland satisfactions to the East Coast. "The scenery around the foothills," he wrote of the same Catskills, "resembles the rolling topography of central Wisconsin." Besides, Joe Jefferson, the great American actor, gave Rip enough of a reality in the last decades of the nineteenth century to draw Hine, interested in wooded nature and young expectations, to Rip's cache. Hine loved Nature's expectations. The next year he returned to Oshkosh, married Sara Rich, and carried her back with him to his urban-natural world of expectation.

Meanwhile he had been working at Ethical Culture School in New York City. Frank Manny, who had been head of Oshkosh Normal and first suggested Hine come east with him, was Superintendent at The Ethical Culture School and employed Hine to teach Botany and Nature Studies. That was in 1901. In 1903 he put a camera in his hand, suggested he use it to teach students . . . and unknowingly extended Hine's vision.

Later it was clear that Hine always thought of himself as a teacher—teacher of children, teacher of adults, teacher of workers, teacher of corporations. Teacher because he let life filter through him and used the

17

word "interpret" to communicate what he was talking about. He had "interpreted school life" he wrote in the '30's, trying to recapture his beginnings, just as he spoke of interpreting "the vast industrial scheme in the 20's." In 1906 he wrote while talking of trees, "A good photograph is not a mere reproduction of an object . . . it is an interpretation of Nature." Although he left classroom teaching in 1908—sliced it completely out of his life—he never cut teaching or interpreting out of his conceptual framework. He felt compelled to arrange his experience for his audience. Hine forever interpreted—nature to children, evils to adults, workers to themselves, the Tennessee Valley to its exploiters. To grasp at some fundamental conflict out of which flowed an abundance of energies and unfold it for others to see, Hines closed in upon a scene. Although the term "interpretive photography" jarred the art photographers, it opened Hine's perspective. He saw a natural-urban image gradually emerge, occupying more and more space in this fast advancing age the twentieth century brought. Hine had to interpret it. When he first received a camera he photographed nature in Central Park in New York City.

In 1905 Hine received his Pd.M. in Sociology from Columbia University in New York City, and met Arthur Kellogg, a Ph.D. student at the School of Social Philosophy. Arthur, Hine recalls, introduced him to social welfare, then to his brother Paul; and with Manny on the one hand and the two Kelloggs on the other, Hine entered the new New York City world.

By 1906, the public had already multiplied, and plunging into that "great public" as he, too, called it then, Hine taught and wrote, touching upon social organization, curriculum, light, charity, Botany, and how and what children learn. At Ethical Culture Hine had a camera club—and then a camera class. Paul Strand, one of Hine's students, remembers that Hine first introduced him to the camera and Alfred Steiglitz. While still teaching, Hine photographed with Charles F. Weller's Washington slum study, went to Ellis Island, wrote about children taking photos on a ferry, photographed for the Charity Organization Society, and also became staff photographer for the *Survey—* then *Charities and Commons* magazine. He created a pattern that bounced with the same intense and often disconnected activity that the new public created. Although the random movements of any person trying to find how he would shape his life, they also reflect the rambling formlessness of that society. In 1908 Hine decided.

He resigned from his teaching post, and took on a monthly appointment as an investigator and cameraman for the National Child Labor Committee. By December of 1908 after having exposed glass works in Indiana and West Viriginia, night markets in Ohio, cotton mills in North Carolina—although the "impetuous and imperious Florence Kelly had no use

18

whatever for photographs in social work, because they had tried it and been discredited"—Hine's photographs revealed a reality no one had seen before. Florence Kelly was the first to say so. Introducing Hine's photos to *Charities and Commons* readers, she wrote, "The camera is convincing. Where records fail and parents forswear themselves, the measuring rod and the camera carry conviction." Although Hine moved through a chaotic tumble of events in the century's first public movements, and, like the decade, had wandered aimlessly about, life crystallized for him in front of the camera.

Once he resigned from his teaching post in 1908, he barely used the written word again. Everything he saw, thought, and interpreted funneled through his photographs. "If I could tell the story in words," he reflected in a letter to Paul Kellogg in 1922, "I wouldn't need to lug a camera."

Addressing a social work conference in 1909 and using stereopticons to illustrate, Hine said, "Whether it be a painting or photograph, the picture is a symbol that brings one immediately into close touch with reality . . . In fact, it is often more effective than the reality would have been, because, in the picture, the non-essential and conflicting interests have been eliminated." Furious at the artist Burnes-Jones who once said he could not paint again if he saw "hopeless lives that have no remedy" Hine frothed, "What a selfish, cowardly attitude!" Placing Victor Hugo's ideas before

his audience he added, "the great social peril is darkness and ignorance . . . Light is required. Light! Light in floods!"

Even his style reflects this. Where impressionist use of light had predominated and Hine had earlier talked of using the "simpler" notion of a silhouette to get effects, once he moved fully into camera investigation, varying tones and more complex balances typified his work. Two and three sources of light rather than a diffuse or obvious tonality highlighted his subjects. Background moved against foreground.

From 1908 on, Hine was backed by the rampant and continual rumble of activities. Sales and activities increased.

McClure's bought. *Everybody's* commissioned work. Charles Edward Russell introduced some of his photographs. He had already photographed for some of the *Pittsburgh Survey* volumes; the Russell Sage Foundation asked him to photograph for *West Side Kids*. Later *World's Work* published others. His photo company's catalogue listed over 1,000 entries, he made slides for conferences, sold to picture services, and worked throughout the second decade for the National Child Labor Committee. Like the decade through which he moved, he developed a characteristic power.

What was particular and local grew. No grand national judgment swept opinions up. Though we use the word "social" and think of a generalized sweep of reform encompassing the early century's rambling

19

thought and movement, separate ideologies springing from separate groups erupted all over the country. Particular organizations, people, and ideals grew and power grew from each. One organization dedicated itself to saving babies. Another to prohibiting liquor. Another to paving streets. Still another to lighting those streets. "Civic" overshadowed "social" in this great new public arena displaying a new society. Each expected to create enough power out of its momentum, not always to change anything; often to conserve. But each expected to create a power out of *its* existence . . . and in effect each helped maintain the singularity of itself.

Even anti-immigrant feeling was individual. Henry James hated the immigrants. They lived off the life-blood that nourished him and he found them disgusting and slimy. Physically revolted at the thought of their invading his way of life—as if he had to physically expand his own person to let them in, he felt like throwing up. Ingurgitating he called it. Though in fact they lived in filth he never visited, in his mind they lived within his world. They were inside him—his world, his America. They were a part of his world and he hated them in his way. One coherent unit of thought did not exist. Many anti-immigrant feelings did. Some wanted to restrict immigration. Others suggested a twentieth-century version of a head tax. The decade fostered the growth of particular units and fed them into some central arena where one saw that virile new public spilling over with strange new growths.

Small-towners became city dwellers and old Victorian city dwellers became new industrial city dwellers. An old morality streamed into the new menage and added its face. Contained wooded naturalism became explosive industrial naturalism. All clashed and a child repeatedly appeared in the center.

Whenever and however one looked life seemed to center about the child. The factory owner, the educator, the prohibitionist, the reformer—all focused on the child. Educators revolutionized the curriculum children were to experience in school. Prohibitionists abhorred children learning sin from the streets. In the canneries, "the goods are perishable and must be put up immediately!" Might not the child labor alongside his mother as she worked in a cotton mill, the mill owner argued. Child labor reformers protested the padrone who brought children "down here to the Gulf in the winter and took them back up to the berry fields in Maryland and Delaware in the summer," condemned the mill owner who laughed at age restriction and grew infuriated with the parent who permitted— no, encouraged—child labor. "Child slavery" a National Child Labor Committee report called it. If anything seemed to draw groups together, if anything seemed to present a beacon for the separate movements it was the sheer existence of and hope for children. As recipients, doers, beholders, as pre-existential beings children

20

became the focus of life. In 1906 A. J. McKelway wrote, "the golden age of the world . . . is still in the future . . . and the central figure on that canvas is that of the little child."

Scanning the particularities of the society as they stretched in front of him, seeing his old Wisconsin woodland, smiling with his Catskill dream, intent upon his new industrial naturalism, seeing the new reality through his camera, watching the continually widening horizon the cityscape suggested, Hine turned to adults and spoke about children. Educating the new public, he photographed and spoke about children—in mills, markets, tenements, farms, schools, shacks. He saw them running, eating, playing, selling, moving, sailing; on streets, beds and sidewalks.

Hine joined with the child labor reformers, was moved by their designs and interests, even helped explain some of their aims. But he always spoke from behind his camera with a power he particularly created. Look at his photographs. Each child is named, placed, and aged. Olga cried as she sat on her house steps. Rose asked Hine to "photograph her dolly too," and Mary "tends the baby when not shucking." Each cotton mill in New Hampshire or North Carolina becomes distinct, each child and his work defined. The individuality with which he saw people, factories, hillsides, machinery, gates, tenements, remains in the photographs. When the photographic world was still engrossed with impressionist lighting, when the salons and the competitions lamented the prevalence of single tones, when some of the reform world objected to the lack of obviousness in a Hine photograph—the lack of overt horror or dispute, Hine "interpreted" the bits and pieces about him as he saw them.

Roger Baldwin remembers Hine gathered with everyone else at the *Survey* office in New York—or even in St. Louis. But Hine was often off by himself—"not communicative about his views or interests," so enmeshed with the "photographic task of the moment" was he. He remembered particular children he met and visited them when he happened to return to the same mill. When he wanted to interpret a worker to himself or to a corporation, he tried to shape a personality at the machine. And when he was hired by the Tennessee Valley Authority to photograph the Clinch Valley before Norris Dam waters would inundate it, he insisted there not be the "usual blare of publicity" because his work was "personal and in places, confidential." More than anything else his sense of individuality guided him and cut precisely into the scene he saw.

Mr. Ralph McDade, presently the Associate Resource Development Specialist at the University of Tennessee and then a fledgling employee of the TVA, remembers escorting Hine through the Valley. Sorghum-making, he tells us, takes a perfect control of temperature throughout the process. Disturbances can affect the total product and the makers are reluctant to relinquish or even re-distribute any time. Yet "Mr.

Hine secured their permission and cooperation." (See photo on page 151) He gained cooperation even as "mixed feelings amongst the residents (toward) any stranger who came into the area ran high . . . When a photographer came, this added to their concern. Mr. Hine . . . was completely comfortable as he dealt with these Tennessee hill folks." To approach people and situations individually was simply Hine's basic operating mode. Sometimes explicit; often an unexpressed fiery existence beneath the surface: no matter, it drove him.

When Henry Hoyt Moore wrote in *Outlook* of the uncluttered lines the new Albright Gallery in Buffalo presented as it opened to the public in 1904, he praised it for its individual approach to design. Having broken with the lines Victorian Gothic had produced, it posed a classic majesty—in an industrializing turmoil-ridden world. Moore thought he saw individuality in the design because of its break with what was. More probably its individuality stemmed from the almost iconoclastic notion that one could assume a classic stance in a world bubbling with change. The particularity that sharpened Hine's view of situations came out of the same early decades that shaped the Albright's.

Some of Hine's most eloquent photographs are of children—individual children classicly posed in a world bubbling with change—a boy leaning on a machine, a boy standing, a young Jewish immigrant. Hine saw the child become the resolution of aesthetic and historic conflict. As if they were the purest flowers a transplanted Nature could cause to grow, Hine's children become classic statements. They fuse rational and moral conviction, especially his conviction that in this new age one should be able to find laboring contentment in the city, that new growth was natural, that it needed only to flower under its own power—especially as these grew. Child labor was an evil. Cut down the evils and let the children grow.

To locate the evils and find the hidden purity, Hine traveled from North to South and East to West mainly between 1908 and 1916. New England cotton mills. New York City tenement-home workers. Baltimore canneries. Carolina mills. Biloxi fishing boats. St. Louis streets. Colorado beet fields. California canneries. Wisconsin cranberry bogs. He visited families at home, read Bibles for birth dates, measured heights of children against his suit coat buttons, and when he was not allowed into factories, waited outside to photograph the leave-taking or the 5 a.m. dimness that started children on their day. To Hine the *demi-monde* seemed a step away.

His anger grew as the "Captains of Industry" found new "tasks for the tots to try." "It is perfectly obvious that our children must be reared in an atmosphere of work," Hine wrote with tongue-in-cheek, "if they are to become Captains of Industry, and so we outdo the Montessori System itself . . . Did I say tasks?" he writes in a report for the National Child Labor Committee in

1914. "Not so—they are 'opportunities' for the child and the family to enlist in the service of industry and humanity. In unselfish devotion to their homework vocation, they relieve the over-burdened manufacturer, help him pay his rent, supply his equipment, take care of his rush and slack seasons, and help him to keep down his wage scale. Of course they must accept with cheery optimism the steady decline in wages that inevitably follows in the wake of homework. Isn't it better anyway for everyone to be working instead of expecting father to do it all?" How cynical could the new industrial world become?

Hine despaired of the crushed dreams an immigrant child more than any other child might experience. When a mother announced "Annie can shuck eight pots a day. Then some other child beats the record," Hine wrote, "Think of a mother urging a girl of her age on to more work . . . Can we call that Motherhood? . . . The baby at Ellis Island little dreams what is in store for him." Like Isaac in Ernest Poole's story *Aristotle and Isaac,* who dreams of coming to America where the machines will make him freer, Hine wanted any American child to be freer because of the new machines. Hine projected his expectations for children onto the constantly expanding society. But an immigrant child, because he was new to the country as well as new to the century, should grow even more explosively in the new society. Although Isaac symbolized Hine's expectation for laboring contentment in the new city, an urban immigrant child personified a perfected expectation for the age.

"Should" was a part of Hine. Morality counted. In an age where the public spoke of knowing what its servants were doing, Hine spoke of these do-ers as Servants of the Common Good. An age-old Protestant concern infused his new urban expectation. One served the new public as one had served God. In addition to a rational and naturalist-scientific expectation that arose out of the transformation of a woodland threshold into a machine-dominated society, a now-secularized formerly religious but still rigorous morality dictated to Hine. It was wrong and sinful for children to be shooting craps out in the street at 1:00 a.m. That their work was inefficient, that they did not learn—these were parts of an unmanageable even inflammatory argument. But underneath that indignation his view of children working screeched with sin. "He knows saloon life, he gambles, he wastes his money . . . The messenger boy carries notes between a prostitute in jail and a man in the red light district." Child labor needed abolition because it was inefficient and irrational. Also because it was wrong. Children belonged under a protective wing. Perhaps within the same enclave where he protected so much of himself.

The era's anger, its murmurings and arguments found no direction. No organization molded its expansive energies. No grand hegemony molded its separate moralities and convictions. But the growing conflicts in

Europe and the just-resolved conflicts of the Russo-Japanese War drew attention to a human being's strength in war. William James articulated these concerns, infuriated at the lack of strength and formless direction his society seemed to display. Blending the first decade's separate concerns into one moral outlook, James urged the many publics facing him to use the same energy they might use in war to create a superior society in peace. Expansively strewn ideals might be gathered into a major force of creative strength. Morality might become a reality. Man had but to create as strongly for these as he does in war. Moral strength, not passive acceptance: these James argued to a public still listening.

To extinguish weakness, to blot out passive goodness and transform it into a martial-like parade, to make goodness a steel-driven creation rather than a weak defense, James spoke of "inflaming the civic temper," of creating a moral conviction akin to the strength a man marshals for war. Hine stood ideologically next to him and wished that a man's more passive woodland components could be transplanted to the urban industrial "martial" scene. Hine photographs appeared both the month before and the months after William James' article, "The Moral Equivalent of War," appeared in *McClures* in 1910, a symbolism we may like to play with. Twenty-two years later Hine quoted from James' piece in his *Men At Work* and wrote of the "constructive conquests of peace-time" in a statement he wrote for the TVA. He then wrote to Paul Kellogg and called this his "credo."

Meanwhile in the early decades, educational theory approached the new urban-natural child and through curriculums, techniques and methods shaped a new program for the child moving into an industrialized golden age. Curriculum developments were unique; but the setting was not to be ignored. For the most direct and most central inheritor of the new urban-natural setting, learning in the path of Fresh Air was best. Fresh Air Schools caught this child-aware world's fancy. Huddled in coats and breathing 5° air, a child could infuse his mind with Math, Science, and English while his body received invigorating stimuli from the fresh-blown wind. The first Fresh Air school opened in Chicago in 1904, and if one lived in New York, one could go in 1910. Nature—earlier or later—could only benefit the mind and body.

More basically, curriculum designs tried to meet the child's natural self-expression. Locked within him—as locked within the new smoke and steel-stacked city—was a positive creative force; and like the city's positive creative energies it was a natural entity and could be encouraged and drawn out. Released, it would contribute to the decade's natural-urban flow. Self-expression for the new city child became an educational goal.

Further, what better place for a child of this new century to find his self-expression than in the laboratories and workshops the new century spawned? Industrial education opened the future, made available the present, and was part of a natural flow from out of the past. Industrial education was like a Golden Egg. Walking from Nature's old garden in the nineteenth century to the untold bounties of the twentieth, a child would naturally peer into vocational education, and should he stop, find there at least a spiritual wealth. "Learning by doing," a child would satisfy his natural instincts to learn. Being a mechanic in this age still meant being an artist. Just as reformers concerned themselves with detail, so too could a child. By taking part in any "doing" activity, he joined his instincts to the rhythms of the new industrialism. Vocational education was the base upon which a flowering enlightenment could grow in the cities. Through it children would come to tower.

When Hine wrote about deaf-mutes in 1908, he talked of the "industrial training" they should have. "Training in accuracy is begun very early ... And surely all this training will serve as a practical and humane enlargement." When a child labor reformer tried to convey the horror of child labor—"what can they know of home when they leave at six in the morning and return at six in the evening?" he suggested they learn first, then work. School gardens even grew out of the desire for industrial education. Oats, peas, and beans grown from seed nurtured by the new city child, plowed by hand, seemed to represent the products of the natural experience turned out of the city.

In 1910 Hine photographed a school garden that ran right up to the fence of a steel mill. Industrial education became one of the shiny gold coins highlighting the period's alacritive edges. It refracted the denial of human fruition but accepted an urban-industrial expectation. The child of that golden future might arise.

Hine himself continued to work in a tumultuous world. The Russell Sage Foundation published "West Side Kids" with Hine photographs. Hine photographed millinery workers for Mary Van Kleeck. He photographed department store workers, new tenement houses. With Belle Israels who later became the Belle Moscowitz of Al Smith's life, he did a story on recreational facilities for working girls. He met Frances Perkins.

But by 1914, after seven years of investigating and photographing children at work, despair seems to have seeped insidiously into Hine. Children still picked nut meats and stitched dolls dresses in the home. In a pamphlet entitled *Tasks for the Tenements* Hine says, "tenement homework seems to me one of the most iniquitous phases of child-slavery that we have. It is then that I come nearest to hysterics, and so, if I seem to be smiling over the subject at any time this morning, you may rest assured I would rather weep." Satan could never "find mischief for Johnny and Jennie to do" —so fully occupied rather than spent in "fruitless play" were they. The "high cost" of child labor still threw children onto a human junk pile. And if in North

25

Carolina the minimum working age went up one year for girls—to fifteen—a prominent manufacturer still wanted to install knitting machines in the homes of the workers. To annex the homes! Education had made no apparent dent. To whom had he been interpreting? How far-away Hine's hopes for self-expressive fruition must have seemed; how foreign his hopes for the child of the century must have become. And one wonders how much his turn toward Playgrounds Association and his photographs of city kids on the West Side result from a kind of dead end. Reform may have gone as far as it could.

World War I broke out in Europe while Hine was still concerned over this country. But increased war talk shaped some of his energies. He photographed army camp training for *Everybody's*. He hoped the Red Cross would use him, matter-of-factly accepted its improbability in 1917, and then was delighted to leave for France in May of 1918, a Captain in the American Red Cross. His employment record does not indicate whether he was or was not married. And of course he was.

Sara Rich Hine had traveled with him to Virginia in 1911. Their son was born in 1912. But she rarely entered his public life—just as, in effect, he himself rarely became personally involved in the outside world. Intense and shy, he abandoned his self-containment under the stimulus of particular ideas. "Let's have lunch some time," he often suggested to Paul Kellogg or Savel Zimand—or any one of his friends. But no sooner had he written the words than he usually added, "It's a busy week coming, so I may not see you right away." First venturing, he then drew back. He grew angry and excited over issues. But however public, however involved a face of him became, he withdrew and retreated. With Homer Folks, the Charity Commissioner of New York, we know that Hine often visited; and although many—if not all—of Folks' business dates appear in his journals, nowhere is Hine mentioned. Did an older Victorian personality contain both and each of these men? Did a small-town circumscribed definition of "private" from "public" prescribe behavior? After Sara Rich Hine died in 1939, Hine wrote to Paul Kellogg that he did not seem "able to make the necessary adjustment," that she was so much a part of his life. This from a man who never mentioned her during this great public life, many of whose colleagues in 1939 had never met her.

Hine protected himself—probably with his graflex exclusively—as he stormed through public life. After six months in France, Hine was attached to the Special Survey Mission Homer Folks headed to investigate the war damage on people and land in South Eastern Europe and Northern France and Belgium. Leaving Paris on November 11 as the Armistice festivities broke out all over the city, they arrived in Southeastern Europe in November. Folks wrote to his wife in Paris on December 13, 1918, "I don't think Hine was ever so happy in his life as here. Something new every minute that he wants to snap. He is out all day picking up interesting things on every hand." Hine was happiest when he was creating. These photographs climactically express the individuality he found in the continually multiplying world. When he returned, he moved in a different direction.

But there is more out of these first few decades. For as Hine moved through that public world he passed through an artist-photography world, picking up and developing from it. He never was of it, just passed through it as he moved and passed through all of his other worlds, never personally involved in any.

It is easy to say that because of newspapers' and magazines' now extensive use of plates, because of the century's new use of cameras, and because the "scientific" nature of the camera matched the new machine-filled image of the twentieth century, Hine attached himself to that movement. It would be easy to assume that a kind of tidal wave of machine-reflected life washed him ashore with it all. But Hine started out with an interest in wood sculpture. Somebody else put a camera in his hands, and by 1906 while he was infused with fiery notions of social welfare, he already had written a piece on silhouettes for *Photographic Times*. He had not even killed off his many old ways of life when he already embarked on a new. What was happening all about him certainly affected him. To

make it causal denies him and beclouds his revolutionary impact.

Look at the man. However much he moved through "public" worlds and however much he became and thought and acted as a "public" figure, he stayed inside his personal world perfecting his craft by himself. Although he brought his camera class to meet Steiglitz and view the Photo-Secessionists' work, according to Paul Strand he never brought his own work to be viewed by Steiglitz. He wrote that schoolchildren should read about photography and become involved in its learning; yet when the great debate over "insurgents" and "regulars" raged over the Buffalo Fine Arts Academy photo show in 1910, Hine took no part.

Yet Hine used artistic standards and measures. Hine was conscious of a photography world: "Reading in the current photo literature (provides) new ideas on process and product," he wrote in the *Photographic Times* in 1908. But he was most conscious of the standards an art world presented: "good photography is a question of art," he added. Raphael provided a model of composition, and Hine told his students how he modeled his tenement Madonnas on Raphael's. He ignored much of what passed through the photographic world and guided himself through the art world. But it was the classic, not the current. Perhaps the classic seemed all the more real in changing times.

He referred to his women and children as madonnas, let halated light through just above the horizon line and balanced groups evenly against each other, especially in some of his early photographs, to highlight the subject in the middle. He relied on this classical composition and captioned many of his photographs as madonnas. While Steiglitz's influence in that period was against any and all restraints—Hine moved within apparently normal and acceptable channels. Classic composition suited him.

By 1910 a conflict between the Steiglitz Photo-Secessionists and the Fraprie-led professionals vied for the term "insurgent." Who was insurgent and who was regular? Both groups were concerned with impressionist lighting. Arguments over gum prints involved both groups. But Hine, off on a completely independent course, viewing his subjects with an intuitively classic approach, sliced into life unaware. His focus was sharper. Light entered the photograph from two and sometimes three sources. Suddenly he disregarded the old classical balance and he strung people together in converging lines that shaped a group at the bottom right of a photograph, broke into emptiness in the middle, set two other groups hovering about, and laid piles of pebbles and grains of wood and patterns of fences to move the eye. Never dramatically: a fence never overpowers, no part upstages another part. Light, line, and form all move with a new balance, molding a new scene for eyes that never before viewed those people at that place in time. He never conceived of his work being revolutionary.

The parallels between Hine's vision of a scene and Picasso's view of a man become stark.

From each angle and from a new plane and perspective Hine broke into what was formerly of one piece and whole. From the side, back, top—as Picasso probed the inner workings of a man—Hine set person against door, brick, or walk, and probed the inner compositions of a scene. Just as Picasso revealed a person from each of many angles, Hine now revealed a scene from each of many angles. As a girl walks into a doorway, one sees the scene through her. But balancing her stance is a sun-lit doorway—and that becomes an angle of entry, a way of looking into the new scene. In front, left, a man stolidly sits, stares out at the audience—and his stare becomes a point of entry, a way of looking into that scene. One sees front through him, sideways through the door, and obliquely through the girl. That she is so within shadow while emerging as the crucial figure pulls the compositional balance in her favor. Just as one looked into a Picasso painting from an eye-opening left, a piercing mouth, or an explosive face, one now looked into a Hine with a cut-off side or a deadened smile. Angles that had never before entered a photograph now did. The huge new multiple society suddenly laid bare its face.

He also dangled emotions and clashed feelings through placement. Sometimes a foreground group balanced the counterpoint a background suggested—as in so many of the waiting-in-front-of-the-factory scenes. Often a fence carried on the rhythm the fore-ground set in motion. Sometimes the background received the impact then dispelled it amidst the machinery. And often a foreground figure creates an emotion opposite to a background figure only to have a fence carry the fiery results away. The subtleties run swiftly —and many have likened his suasions to Atget, one a contemporary of the other, neither probably having seen the other or the other's work.

As far as we can tell, Hine never consciously analyzed the scene we now see before he photographed it. It existed and he saw it. If his photographs sometimes bear an existential flatness—a "pure" malaise of the continuing human condition—it is because acceptance sits restively within his photographs. Hine subjects apparently accept their malaise yet continue to convince us they live—not thrive, just exist and not die. This drained pre-existential flatness results from an insistent and absolute commitment, not withdrawal. Though personally removed from the "public" he was made alive by these publics, not deadened by them.

He consciously saw the particularities of the malaise. Finding place for a small-town Victorian tone of religiosity as he joined the "divine beauty of form" to an industrial world, he quoted George Eliot, the nineteenth-century novelist, as he spoke to the Conference of Charities and Corrections in Buffalo in 1909.

Paint us an angel, if you can, with floating violet robe and a face paled by the celestial light; paint us a Madonna turning her mild face upward, and opening her arms to welcome the divine glory, but do not impose on us any esthetic rules which shall banish from the reign of art those old women with work-worn hands scraping carrots, those heavy clowns taking holiday in a dingy pothouse, those rounded backs and weather-beaten faces that have bent over the spade and done the rough work of the world, those homes with their tin pans, their brown pitchers, their rough curs and their clusters of onions.

It is needful we should remember their existence, else we may happen to leave them out of our religion and philosophy, and frame lofty theories which only fit a world of extremes. Therefore, let art always remind us of them; therefore, let us always have men ready to give the loving pains of life to the faithful representing of commonplace things, men who see beauty in the commonplace things, and delight in showing how kindly the light of heaven falls on them.

Photography could light up darkness, expose ignorance. Out of an emotional reserve that found its public light through the camera only, Hine consciously pursued a role as a social photographer.

Hine revamped and injected excitement into what he had passively received from the photography world. In January of 1908 an article entitled, "De Kid Wot Works At Night" appeared in *Everybody's Magazine*. Photographed by Emmet V. O'Neill, it portrays, in spite of its title, a generally unsentimental layer of street life. Many photographs resemble—some have an

29

uncanny resemblance to—Hine's photographs. A newsboy against a lamp-post. Another inside a hash-house. A shoeshine boy at night. But in looking more closely the Hine parallel fades, for as Hine closed in on a similar scene he changed the view from vertical to horizontal, relit the subjects, and suspended judgment on the individuals. A year after Steichen took his portrait of J. P. Morgan, Hine took the Jewish immigrant on Ellis Island, the immigrant's hand, as J. P. Morgan's hand, separately lighted, too. George O'Hara photographed people in tenements mostly in Buffalo, Jessie Tarbox Beals photographed slums—and cats—in New York. And a Brown Brothers photograph—as if dropping a Rip Van Winkle pellet within Hine to awaken his sensibilities 20 years later—depicted a construction worker out on a steel beam over the city. Most of the other photographers realistically spread an era's subject in front of the magazine audience. Steichen still echoed the photography world's clouded light—as in his portrait of Victor Berger. Hine's photographs provoked an audience.

30

Hine could not live in the world of photography. The Photo-Secession group experimented and incited, but within defined limits. It attracted those interested in furthering photography as an art form—as well of course as those looking for a particular place and station in the photography world. Clarence White exhibited with them. Charles Ogburn, Paul Strand, Imogen Cunningham: all devoted their perceptions to photography and a perfected statement of that art form. The group drew newcomers; it was not a closed status group. It did more than any other group or movement to implant photography as an art form in the public eye. But it did not provide the haphazard exciting raw-edge—unfinished, but compelling—that an individual like Hine needed.

Hine lived on that edge. Protected by his camera, utterly committed, Hine looked for blatant life. He searched where he was not wanted, photographed where the owner objected, and found the word "detective" described the work that pushed him into continually new conflicts.

The art world taking shape was stabler and less infusive. Though we know the changes the Ash Can School represented began in the first decade and even know that Glackens, Henri, and Luks turned their attention to the new urban subjects and a new somber mood, we also know that they rocked no boat and provoked no drastic fling. Lighting remained essentially the same, composition did not vary and if the new photography clashed over which group held the avant-garde toe-hold, the art world still fought for place in respectability. It was safer to visit the heights the past created. New modes were established within reach of the past.

The general magazine world was even more completely a product of the past. What had been a complex array of light streams in the mid-nineteeenth century, what had been the source of Impressionism's birth, merged into a single stylized "public" source of light by 1904. A dreamy undefined wisp of light swept across the pages of *Scribner's* magazine as Edith Wharton described her heroine running across the street. On other pages filmy hair and a suggestion of steps carried the heroine quickly behind the door her lover was about to open. Bathed in clouds of gray fading light, horrified faces ready to shout or proclaim flowed from page to page. What had been an original and creative use of light to begin with lapsed into a mass stylization gripping its viewers to easy shock and apparent sensibilities. What had originally upset and unnerved now just titillated. Readers relaxed back after finishing, never having been stirred out of their comfort.

Art and History constantly run with each other. One cannot be substituted for the other. But the most perfect—the most telling and refined—artistic statement becomes also the most perfect historic statement. How the included details are shaped, how the shape takes form: these minute historic facts become the basis of the artistic conflict. The artistic conflict Hine creates in a photograph comes right out of the living conflict he saw. The "purity" of a child and the "natural" expression with which his dammed-up reserves could best spill over: these Hine posed against the factories and fences. Artistically and historically *that* child conflicted with *that* gate. The movement the child generated in real life provided the basis for the movement he gen-

erated in a Hine photograph. Somewhere within his private world on his side of the camera, Hine saw that boy smilingly stride up to the factory, his photographic-artistic movement caught by the shadowy receding figure, the post-after-post fence finally dispelling that artistic movement and leading it right out of the photograph. This is a photograph of child labor. It catches the historic truth—the recesses and acceptance. The eye wants to resolve it artistically.

Conflicts are essential to artistic expression. Whether it is the conflict the wind creates as it blows a still flower, the conflict a person creates as he steps out of a secular fountain of religiosity—as in Renaissance expression—or the conflict an age creates resisting the power it has created, conflict composes the representation figures into some sort of spatial arrangement. Hine built the artistic conflict out of the historic conflict he saw around him, making his humans correspond to the humans he saw. Often emotions vie with each other, as in the photograph where the little boy strides up to the factory gate smiling while a huddled figure cynically crowds out his burst of emotion, only to have the picket fences run out of the photograph carting all spent emotion away. Sometimes backgrounds vie with foregrounds directly, as in a textured hillside filled with clam shells upon which children carry shrimp pails. Or sometimes the background vies with the foreground only to throw the impact right back upon the foreground, as in the photograph of the beggar woman standing in front of a New York City subway-elevated entrance. There the horse faintly outlines a background only to re-enforce the hesitant woman. The life each photograph generates communicates directly to us, perhaps about ourselves. We see and learn history from a Hine photograph, but we're concerned with the people and their feelings. The artistic conflict triggers our eye.

How much did Hine "see"? How much "luck" entered the scene? Any good photographer constantly talks of "luck", for the field of vision, especially in a view camera, does not duplicate the filmed image. What turns up on the film could just as easily not turn up—as far as precise judgments are concerned. But Hine so consistently framed a scene in the same way that that pattern of "luck" frames our view of his work. He organized people rather "simply" in front of the camera. A whole group lined up outside the factory gate and Hine presumably came along and simply caught them as they were. But once our eye starts into the photo, it continues, weaving across the heads grouped in the lower right, stopping off center at the factory gate entrance, and then running out at the top left. A high degree of order apparently rests inside and between these groupings, enough to propel the viewer's eye more swiftly and evenly than he is aware of. It's more than luck; at least a pattern. Of course to Hine the significant fact about each photograph was the statement he made. Anything more than that statement

probably remained irrelevant. He trained his eye to make that statement more perfectly. His public reacted; and Hine felt buoyed by the range of response and accord it offered.

Each particular conflict Hine abstracted probably represented a timeless human conflict more than he ever suspected; and as we see these same photographs today, the movement that was locked within the historic reality seems to be spilling out. Gyorgy Kepes, the Hungarian-born artist and art critic, speaks of a composition starting life with an "unsaturated" structure—just a basic linear flow to direct the eye from group to group. The best structures, though, he tells us, "fill up" as new human experiences add new dimension to the composition. A Hine photograph—unsaturated to begin with—appears more filled today. Today's experiences add to the figures in the photographs, and artistic movement that ran rather "simply" between planes in 1910 now runs in excited patterns. The "simple" or "primitive" organization of people in front of the camera that ordered a past chaos held explosive feelings intact. Today's human wants—not tangible wants—pry open those explosive feelings and spread them all over the photograph. Within that "random" order, Hine abstracted a meticulous expression of continuing human conflict; triggered by the years of new life, that expression flows from group to group. A Hine photo is more filled with movement and conflict today than when it was taken.

Art and history each draw upon human composition. The people seem more real, more pervasive even after the passage of years. The settings pungently balance and unbalance, revealing the figures more fully. Finally both the soul and the face of the photograph become real.

The truthfulness of any art, the degree of honesty it can communicate, becomes its agelessness. The most perfect abstractions that can creep into a representational form is what flows out of that art form in later epochs. Unsaturated to begin with, the art form receives the impact of age upon age. Movement that runs between two planes begins to fill up more and more space. It sweeps across the planes and becomes grander. The gap between what was explicitly stated in one age and what a later age takes out becomes narrower. Art becomes the perfection of the past. The most perfect artistic representation orders the most perfect form of the lines and space and people and light that occupy that time and space in history. Only the best art can order the chaotic tumble of events. Only the best can re-align chaos to suggest both the chaos and the order it will become.

Out of commitment Hine did this. Not a commitment to art—but out of a commitment to expose the horrors so that the most perfect living order could take shape. Disregarding fashion, Hine broke into the new reality. And just as Picasso used a profile to cut into a whole man, Hine cut off a man and broke into a whole reality. Like Modigliani's technique of cutting off legs to bring the nude right up and at the viewer, Hine's cut-off reality foreshortened perspective and brought the viewer upon the new whole scene. He drove himself personally, innovated artistically. Out of the unquenchable desire to find the most perfect living order, Hine ended up creating a new artistic order.

Hine could only have satisfied himself in an industrial setting. He could only have found the nature from which he grew thriving in the new urban-industrial complex. He had finished being a rural person when he left Oshkosh. How much Dewey at Chicago affected him is conjecture. But he could only have found his fulfilled self—that expression of his private world—amongst the chaos that the early twentieth century created. And he could only have spilled over and re-planted that nature-raised private world in a steel-filled world.

His fulfillment grew out of his unconscious. Just as all order can come only out of chaos—whether it be societal, personal, or artistic chaos—Hine's fulfillment ordered that unconscious, ordered those rambling undefined continuing sub-explicit explorations. Explicitly he sought to stamp out the evils so that the purity of the American urban soul might grow. But implicitly his own "artistic temperament"—referred to by so many in the 30's—his own interior privately motivated, privately defined world needed expression, growth, and fulfillment. Not just a "playing out" in a sample re-

33

gurgitation—to match Henry James' "ingurgitation"—but an enlarged and wider expression of that world. Hine needed to expand. The old natural world could just contain and protect his self-expression. The expanding industrial world received his expanding personal world. His unconscious moved right into the industrial setting, ordering in perceptive insights some of the chaos spread all about, even buoying his conscious commitment.

To some he was an enigma. To others he seemed dynamic. Others conceived of him being warm and friendly. To one seeing all the parts, he must have seemed like a cubist representation—a man with a top, side and bottom, all shrieking for expression and place, each an insight into the new multiple but divisive individual personality. As one conceives of one whole man finally emerging from a Picasso painting, so does one see Hine as a whole complete man finally emerging from the new industrial world. Never from an old comfortable Oshkosh woodland.

In 1939, when he went back over his life to prepare a folio of his work, he talked of the laboring contentment one should have experienced out of the century's industrial rise, of fruition out of work, of fulfillment out of industrialism. Children would serve to create a Golden Age, but the craftsman had a sort of golden age in the palm of his hands, especially the craftsmen in the city. As if the other side to the balance weighted by children, men at work engrossed him. One of his

first photographs, taken in the same year he photographed immigrants on Ellis Island, was of the printer. The singular care the printer exercised, the exactness—and the voluminous background fascinated him. As if tracing the very pattern he made for himself, he gave the craftsman a personal spot in a massive industrial world, enhancing his individuality as he drew him into the erratic and sometimes horrific flicker of the new world.

In trying to explain the motivations of early twentieth-century reformers, some critics have relied on guilt—as if the comfortable backgrounds out of which reformers came would explain their movement onto the edgy, often ugly, rot-gut rim they chose. True or not for others, guilt explains nothing of or about Hine. Hine sought the creation not the re-creation of himself. He tried to identify each of the parts of himself, and to shape them into a meaningful unit. To line up facet A with facet B, to place them in angular regularity, to rearrange and recompose them. This is what Hine tried to do unconsciously. From a wide base he sought to create a new image of himself and a new image in the new America. The angle of vision he created for himself, the lines and limits and outward scope he achieved: these stayed with him for the rest of his life.

Hine entered the future out of the oblique multiplicity of the century's first two decades. Shaped by his expectations and finding place for some of those expectations, he moved into the 20's and later the 30's as

34

if along a prescribed route: it was broad to begin with and he followed its lines. His expansive outlook grew out of the rambling multiple possibilities of those decades and however society's expression of its wants may have risen, Hine thrived on its freewheeling character. He could be definite while it was indefinite. He could order the chaos it created while it supported both his unconscious and conscious mind. It supported both his eye and his commitment.

World War I represented the age's martial expansion, and bizarre though it seems, Hine reached the climax of his expression of the century's humanist expectations in the land and people he found in Europe at the end of the war.

The ghost of the early century's anti-immigrant feeling still hung limply about in 1917 as a country marched off to war. In 1918, an article in *Survey* magazine argued that "Slavs and Italians, foreign born and native born, have worked shoulder to shoulder." Formed in a giant effort to save the world for democracy, cheer leaders—as if on a 50-yard line—repeated the words of unity the war was to have effected. But anti-immigrant feeling grew even more active as words tried to reassure a populace it was really welded together.

In the Spring of 1919 Hine arrived back in Paris with Folks and the rest of their party from the Special Survey Mission to South Eastern Europe. It had taken them into Italy, Serbia, and Greece. After a day or so

recuperating and absorbing the spring-time Parisian flavor they set off on the northern journey through France and Belgium. The Mission was to investigate the effects of the war, the danger, despair and decadence the war had brought. Each leg of the two-part survey has a different feeling about it. Perhaps each area was unique; perhaps a sense of world-wide disaster had arisen just six months after the Armistice. The photographs from South Eastern Europe are full of people, whether screaming, dying, standing, or walking. But hardly a person appears in the Northern France and Belgium series; dust, lifeless land, rubble, fallen buildings, hanging shutters.

Combles (page 122) appears to be completely razed, and according to *Les Guides Bleus* for *La France Nord Et Est* published in 1925, disappeared completely after a fierce battle in 1916. Without combat—and presumably without life of any sort—it was retaken by the Allies in August of 1918, eight months before Hine photographed it. Just as it was possible to read magazines and journals, issue after issue, in the spring of 1919—and especially in April, the month Hine took the Northern survey photos—and read only of reconstruction, repair, rebuilding—the reestablishment of life—one senses total despair in Hine's Belgian photographs. It seems that although the United States had entered and helped fight a war—used men's national spirit to help create a meaning for the word democracy—the country seemed helpless, a spiritual death hung over life.

Hine had caught this mood of despair and after completing the northern leg of his survey he went back to Paris, and by June, after being assigned the care of the money for the mission, allocated the proper amounts— he was paid $300 a month as a photographer and an additional $100 for administering the survey—he returned to New York, checked in with the Red Cross people, and then looked about. Enervated by the humanist resolution of the war, and by his own perceptions, he was eager to start business again. He dropped a note off to Paul Kellogg in June telling him he would continue to use Hiram Meyers' darkroom until he started his up again. Yes, he could handle print orders there. Doubleday prepared a four-page spread of his European photos for *World's Work,* Homer Folks used them in his *Harper* article and book, *Human Costs of the War.* Paul Kellogg used them in *Survey;* and in 1920 he did a fairly spectacular issue on Pittsburgh and steel in *Survey.* When both the National Arts Club and the Civic Club presented a one-man show of his work in 1920 and 1921, it looked as if he had found a direction for the exaltation that he had slid into, the uphill swing the country experienced from out of 1919's floundering.

Reviews were spectacular, even of the conception and place of the show and the building. Hine was the first photographer to have been exhibited by the artists: and his Civic Club show drew praise from *Literary Digest* and the *New York Evening Post.* His base of appreciation was the widest it had ever been. Never having seemed consciously to want praise from the art and photography worlds, nonetheless he received praise from both of them for his sheer artistry. Commitment and artistry, they said, joined in Hine's work. The *Literary Digest* wrote "In his pursuits as a sociological investigator and recorder, Mr. Hine had, whether consciously or not, employed his instincts as an artist." He was at a pinnacle.

Yet right after the show he wrote off to Frank Manny questioning, wondering—no, angered by the absence of an old world. Though maintained by a photography and artistic world of critics, supported by a changed group of institutionalized social welfare critics, and elevated by the widest base he had ever had, Hine was bitter. "Where was Paul?" he wanted to know. Did Paul come and see the show? And what about Spargo, the Spargo who had so clearly reproduced *The Bitter Cry of Children* in 1905? Where were the exponents of life and purpose? And Steiglitz? Did he see and feel the show? Where was the old "fun" he wanted to know, the "fun" that came out of "fundamental"—the sheer joy that comes from creative fulfillment in a growing society? That the total base creating and supporting his show was wider than it had ever been was essentially insignificant. The base that had supported him as a person, that had received and woven and then elevated his private world of expression was now faltering. Hine could not find the same horizon. His angle of entry into the new society did not reveal the same view.

A new national blanket covered the old particularist expectations. Where "civic" and "public" had maintained the separateness of the century's years before the war, now "democracy" and "national" swept it all into a new power-ridden drive. The "public" had always been composed of the many separated parts. Now driven by the century's newly harnessed power, a national overview blotted out distinctions. Even the "weakness" to which both William James and Walter Lippman pointed gave way to a strength. The left-over Victorian particularity that had seemed to find a place in the first part of the century became the new zest-ridden power of the '20's. The potential for power gave way to power itself as multiplicity at the bottom gave way to cohesion at the top. A public became a nation.

And where Hine was educating the "public"—the myriads of people who were creating the great new society in 1912, in 1921 he was educating a more defined column of people: workers and industrial managers. He expected the photographs he took of men in industry—"work portraits" he called them—to document how the worker personally took up the challenge of industrialization. In that same year an economic slump held the about-to-be-flourishing prosperity in check, and Hine wrote to Paul Kellogg that "as soon as the industrial gears grip again, I am sure there will be plenty of progressive industries ready to pay the freight for this kind of publicity and morale." Hine truly expected that his Work-Portraits would help a worker see the beauty and greatness of his work, just as he expected the industrial managers would see—"not (in a) paternalistic" way —how great their force together with an industrial force could be. To make industry and the workers aware of labor's meaningful role, "to link employer and employees in this great method of education," Hine photographed "Men at Work" throughout the decade. How much this grew out of the first decade's natural-urban expectation when men would "no longer (be) members of a single class, but fellow-citzens of one great people." Hine followed the angle his initial entry into the century's urban-industrial image created for him.

At no point did Hine's enthusiasm for reform falter. The "Pennsy people," Hine wrote, "have given me such good cooperation." He wrote to Edgar L. Thorndike at Columbia University suggesting "actual tests to show how these workers compared in general intelligence, etc. with those in the professions and elsewhere." Thorndike was interested. Hine's enthusiasm grew, taking a different form as it moved into the educational layers he thought he saw in the institutions and structure of the new '20's. Swept by his image of the voluptuous nature of the new industrial democracy, Hine expected a groundswell to accompany his show. He wanted people, like his photograph of the printer, to see his show, and feel the unity of life and labor he talked about. If this new nation now sat atop the public that had exposed so many edges, certainly it could harness all the potential power. Industrial power, worker power, and democratic power might become fused into one. "Despite the literal character of much of his work, imagination" streams persistently through it. And the *Literary Digest* adds, "Hine . . . is something of a dreamer." Hine wanted people to like his show for the same reasons he created it. He never thought that perhaps the twenties' high-rise growth eradicated a responsive public.

His angle of vision no longer matched the dominant contemporary angles even though he turned to power and photographed men in turbines, behind generators, and behind the incalculable machine-ridden power producers. He photographed men on rigs, men turning bolts, even an industrial camp where children were being taught to run the new age's machinery. He photographed a slice of the dominant part of the new society and received jobs and acceptance. Some of his work was even pirated—a sure sign of success. During the first part of the '20's *Survey Graphic* issues on Coal, Steel, and Health appeared with Hine photographs—just as Joseph Stella's drawings on cities appeared too in those years. He photographed Al Smith's father for a series on truckmen, J. Walter Thompson's agency seemingly printed some of his work, Burton, Barton, Durstin and Osborne merely used it without credit, Sloan Liniment Ads paid him and the Art Directors Guild awarded him *the* prize for photography in 1924. But he could not find a public. By 1926 the earlier response seems to have petered out. No widespread diffuse but rampant base supported him.

The photographs for the most part are stilted, formalized, and lacking in feeling. Abstractions of reality, they rarely catch reality. An intellectual conflict hangs heavily within each, but real conflict is missing. The artistic order and impending chaos that place so many of his earlier works on a precipice is missing. Hine tried hard to identify with the new society. But the communication he had had with the old public he no longer had with this new institutionally-directed life. His vision no longer matched its vision. That he was like so much of his society seems almost ironic.

Not quite smug, he was too sweet and soft for that. But he was contained, so contained within his expression of this new worker power that he could not see or feel the conflict. For unlike the earlier years where there was less power, and multiple awareness rambled along the bottom levels of the public consciousness, now there was more power and it all ran up the ascents each line of inquiry decreed, the new national conception tying it all together at the top. Like sociology books that talked their own language, and Steichen who photographed fashion, and Steiglitz who saw clouds, and writers who left the country so that they could escape the new narrower and separated confines, Hine probably defined men and machines too confiningly. Once his old base was gone, he lived more passively.

By 1930, Hine felt disjointed . . . as of course the

economy was. He wrote to Paul Kellogg that he was thinking of selling his house and moving to a rural up-state community "where there is more underfoot than 'overhead.'" Perhaps pure Nature was the only source of life for Hine after all. If the counterpointed rhythms of life and labor in the industrial scene could not cradle him in contentment then perhaps the timeless soothing satisfactions of nature could.

He never moved. Instead, in 1930, he recorded the building of the Empire State Building. In close to 1,000 exposures he photographed the men who built it and the structure they created. He caught the towering sensation of mastering both Man and Nature: Man because this building topped all that men had formerly built, Nature because *It* still underlay all. The building symbolized a potential for greatness; it harnessed "productive" energies—a word Hine repeatedly loved and used. And as it climaxed one expression at least of the new century's power, it also matched it with the power a worker gave to the structure—and the age. "I have always avoided dare-devil exploits," Hine wrote after completing his Empire State work, "and do not consider these experiences as going quite that far—but they have given a new zest...and perhaps, a different note in my interpretation of Industry." Hine found "human spirit" in the building as well as experiencing the sheer exciting adventure with power.

But he could not stay on this plane. He could not live with it. He was pushed and pulled up onto the mooring mast of the Empire State, the highest point yet reached on a man-made structure. Though some of the photographs catch the counterpointed rhythms of human and machine-driven life, masterfully exploit the suspension of human and machine-driven conflict, he could not live on that edge. He moved within it as the building was going up, "pictured the imagination and the fleeting moment...brought a new vision to the public" but he could not stay out on the plane of power it suggested. He never moved back to a rural setting, but his best photographs after the Empire State scenes in the '30's are of rural people. Portraits of older people usually, one or two of children; and settings. His conscious self stayed in the city. Personally and artistically, he wandered back to the country.

Why and how did fame falter for "lewhine"—a signature he sometimes loved to use? The pattern and paths his life took move curiously in and out of periods. He thought more highly of his work portraits than he did of his other work and felt proudest of his accomplishments as an industrial and social photographer, as a photographer who interpreted, he hoped, the lifeblood of industry. He devoted more and more time, spirit, and energies to these. If others could see the beauty of the craftsman's work, the economic importance of his existence, and the biological strength of his body, then they would see the new American Man. He was there—the new American Man to parallel the new

American Century. Everybody should see, idolize, and understand his importance; this conception drove him throughout the '20's and into the '30's, taking a huge emotional chunk out of his life.

He tides over into the '30's mainly because of these photographs, and the people who saw them in the '30's link Hine with the present and in effect have prevented his work from being lost. But throughout that period they never saw his best and early photographs. Walter Rosenblum, the head of *Photo League* at the time of its dissolution, the group that inherited Hine's personal effects after his death in 1940, never saw, for instance, most of Hine's child labor and World War I photos. In the '30's one met Hine as a friendly person with an illusory easy-going manner tied to naked and lofty dreams. One saw neither the fire of the man nor the fury from a dimension that produced a timeless expression. Hine stayed alive as a photographer because of a condensed version of his wide-angled vision. He was also often elusive, and as he slipped through his private world, he wrote to Paul Kellogg in the '20's, "I fear me but that is an old story."

Hine's vision from behind his protected camera directed his pursuits throughout his life. The wedge the first decade of the twentieth century opened for him defined the outer limits of Hine's life for him. Like a pyramid, there came a point when the movement within that wedge—ideas, dreams, and man all together—would force itself to a pinnacle. By 1933 that happened. Hine could not see beyond that climax.

Within the first decade, though, as the range and space over which he traveled moved as far and wide as the society underfoot, Hine lived within a sumptuous multi-level world. Committed to realizing a purpose out of establishing himself in the veins of the new industrial century, he worked with both Kelloggs, met Jane Addams, drew comment from Florence Kelly, knew Frances Perkins, worked with Mrs. Belle Israels (Moscowitz) and visited with Homer Folks. His friends came mainly from the reform world. But Hine's search was particularly his. Apart from transplanting a past purity to the new city, Hine's self-expressive insistence continually drove him. Recall Roger Baldwin's comment and look at the unique shape such a scene presented. Consciously Hine was a part of the world of critic-reformers. He could not live without them, and they absolutely hung on his work. But in the center of activity, as conferences took place, Hine shut himself off from them involved with the camera. He lived on many levels even as he focused his energies.

He wrote of techniques, laughed at the off-beat moments a light-hearted journey on a ferry filled with schoolchildren created, fenced himself into the camera world as he cut himself off from the educational world. Yet he never lived in the photographic world. Strand, remember, tells us that as far as he knows Hine never brought a photograph to Steiglitz—an unheard-of phenomenon for a serious art photographer of that day.

40

Photography was personal to Hine. It lived close upon —no, right inside him. But it was a field over and through which he wandered—probably rather shyly even as he worked intensely with the tools it created.

He achieved a height out of those years. By design, Hine consciously sought to order the chaos about him. And he saw that order—even as he overtly and actually sought new order—in the strength of the character of the people he photographed. The artistic design and the new social order he shaped outside a factory gate built itself out of the particular people he saw. Commitment spiraled him, and he stood behind his camera and saw individuals rising out of the century's first years.

1921 started as a spectacular year for Hine. Having been acknowledged in fields of social welfare before World War I, he now received praise from art circles; the worlds of both art and social awareness buoyed and praised him. But the year was short-lived. The nourishment he needed to continue was broken off even though two independent worlds had merged in their focus upon Hine. Purpose and fruition seemed to have vanished. Where the art world remained fairly constant and could support Steiglitz' ventures with clouds, the world of social response lost its solid state to the productive power of the '20's. Who received Hine? Which audience responded? Neither social movements nor art. An industrial world responded. Advertising media picked up his work. And the "fun" he felt so crucially a part of fundamentals—the fruition he felt

out of finding gems in that rot-gut core of life—simply did not exist. In addition to being shy, in addition to being wan, in addition to having built a circumscribed but creative life of a loner, Hine's angle of entry—his guide through life—probably disconnected him more completely than he ever had been by 1929—an awful year to have been totally lost. No wonder that he looked to nature's contentment.

A stream of Hine wandered off from 1918-1919, cut under the '20's, emerged in 1930, and was to continue all through the '30's to provide a thin connection to contentment. When the fundamental world Hine had known failed to expand, failed to spread itself with the productive power of the '20's, Hine turned to the American Red Cross as a source of continual connection. He photographed nurses in the '20's, the drought in 1930, floods in upstate New York in '35, safety techniques, swimming safety, and an endless run of jobs to help them carry on their instructive and aid work. Only the World War I and Drought series furnish great photographs. But that independent stream—so characteristically Hine—as in its line definition—ran as a skeleton behind Hine's dominant moves in the '20's.

Hine closed worlds behind himself. Once he exploited the expressive possibility of a subject he left it. The world of small talk was never his. Hine never let his whole self go out to meet the whole or even a big chunk of the world in which he worked. He lived and worked in water-tight compartments. By 1932 when he published his book, *Men at Work,* presenting his industrial photographs of the '20's to a new world, few knew, remembered, or connected his early child labor photographs to these. Only those people who experienced these photographs at the time they were taken—contemporaries like Baldwin—remembered them. Many of his World War I photos, here reproduced, have never before been printed, much less shown. And many of his photos printed in journals of the first decade no longer exist.

By 1930 the Art Director of *Survey* thought Hine was "old-fashioned" and he was. Even though he lived on a precarious tangent when he photographed the Empire State Building, the flat existentialism that characterized so much of the conflict he posed was passé. Magazine photography in the '30's thrived on the quick jazzy spurts the '20's had unloosened. The candid camera caught a faster pace. And when human concerns were later funneled through the organizational schemes of the '30's a new school of documentary photography grew. Hine was never a part of that. Even when he used some of the newer technical developments—in his TVA series, for instance—he still caught the widest possible base for his photographs, letting his eye wander up and down hillsides and include rambling multiplied detail. The Farm Security Administration, headed by Roy Stryker, developed a working department and out of that a mode of photography. They found dramatically clear sometimes

obvious conflicts and the edges running through those conflicts became brittle and sharp. They reveal life much more immediately; little is imminent. FSA photography developed in part out of the period's urgent contrasts and in part out of Hine. "No photographer in the twentieth century," Ben Shahn has said, "cannot pay heed to Hine." Stryker admired but could not use Hine.

By 1932 Hine was isolated and essentially bitter. When his TVA photos were printed in 1934 in *Survey* with no credit line he assumed malicious intent. "I'd expect Morgan and his Men to be unwilling to acknowledge that those five studies were mine but I am surprised that some *Survey* keen-eye did not notice that there was a considerable Hine accent about them." Insulated against all that was happening, he could not accept—as he had in earlier, easy-going non-crucial relationships with the world—the possibility of an accident.

But he found aspects to connect up to. It looked as if the democracy everyone saw, felt, hoped, or looked for after World War I was rising out of the '20's productive powers and emerging in the '30's. A national and governmental fervor in institutional development, creating institutions of all shapes and sizes, grew all about. Government agencies and private institutions produced a realistic edge of dynamic republicanism as the country began to recover from the Great Depression. Hine connected to fragments that the new world of institutions spun off in the '30's. Mr. Sidney Blumenthal of Shelton Looms saw Hine create a "quasi-reality (out of) its dreams." He photographed for the TVA, spoke of his work with the Rural Electrification Administration, and headed a National Research Project on Manpower for the WPA. But he came to feel only barely comfortable with some of the new age's expressions. Though recommended for a job even though he was a "true artist type"—simply because "the quality of his work is worth it," a letter follows and explains that he "requires some 'waiting upon'." In another instance, Roy Stryker felt he made too many demands to be hired by the FSA. The new national public—not the old particularist public—looked for expression. The '30's sliced off a part of Hine, only a part. Hine stayed within his world, coming out for disjointed singular connections even though the rest of organized America grew with a new humanist fervor.

Earlier, whether he was personally contained or not was irrelevant. He created new images through which the public thought. When he "feared himself" it never affected his vision. Activity characterized him. Once out of focus with his times, though—and Walter Rosenblum, then the "young kid in the Photo League office," remembers Hine sitting off on the side, an onlooker smiling at the intensity and loves that engage young men—a modesty engulfed him and many preferred calling him "shy".

He kept up with the world mainly because he needed money. He lived off photographs. In 1932 he did an excellent run of industrial photographs for Shelton Looms; none are absolutely timeless, but many superbly illustrate industrial moments. To expand his earnings from the series, he tried to sell prints and enlargements to the Metropolitan Museum of Art in New York, the Art School in Daytona, Florida, the Public Library in St. Paul, Minneapolis—to educational and social institutions of all sorts across the country. He was faintly successful. In 1936 he arranged with Ewing Galloway to sell prints from some of his early standard work. He continued to accept series assignments from *Survey Graphic*, traveled extensively for the Manpower Study, sometimes reprinted old photos, and felt a sense of ground-shaking that grew out of the new federated purpose, but never felt swept with its expectation. Rather he connected to it only when his particularist expectations coincided with a moment in its organized momentum. His connections to the '30's most often grew out of jobs and the need for money—many were based on old roots, and he saw, felt and moved only as his own now more thickly insulated self allowed him.

Revived by this work in the later '30's—some of it reminded him of the "old child labor and *real* Red Crossing days"—he still had no intention of really venturing into this new world. After the Empire State, he could not live out on new adventurous tangents. Too unsteady "on the projection a new steel foundation unloosened," too far "off keel," he had no intention of following that or any adventurous fling even should it offer firmer footing. Just "droll" "fundamental" attachments he kept. And with them the probably unrecognizable comfort he felt in his first satisfactions with Nature.

When Hine published *Men At Work,* he prefaced it with a section from William James' "Moral Equivalent of War." For Hine the human condition would have its most flowering embellishments when the infuriating fervor that men could marshal could reshape societies. Though Hine had climbed to the topmost tower of man's mastery over nature and then ambled with man's potential in Nature's garden, though he had memorialized human strength and beauty, though he himself spoke in his TVA proposal of "constructive conquests of peacetime, rather than destructive aggressive acts of warfare," he still searched for the most perfect expression of man's strength. Though by now he was probably only comfortable with pure Nature, he still searched for an expression of human strength in urban industrial as well as natural settings. This search sat inside his insulation, activating, gnawing—never at rest.

He knew he was a pioneer, spoke of his being a "first," proudly assumed the honor of being the first photographer to exhibit at the National Arts Club. He absorbed all these marks of success and wore them with prideful satisfaction. But he was never satisfied for long. Contentment over a long period exploded—not dramatically because he was not a fiery person—but restlessly. He found himself "at sea" after he finished photographing for *Survey Graphic's* Coal Issue. "Even skyscrapers have their basements and skyscraping... its rebounds and depressions," he wrote after completing the Empire State work. And the "old hulk" as he often called himself often seemed to be "drifting" aimlessly about—on that sea.

Some of this growing inability to be satisfied, as if an infectious spread of a disease, was the restless spur that propelled him—and propels all creators. No sooner had he finished with a particular assignment than that restless biting edge began to creep upon and cut into him. In periodic continuum, the "old hulk" would feel tossed by the sea. A part of that edge erupted normally out of the first satisfied scars of completion. But a part did not. Satisfaction could not settle the continual omnipresent edge Hine carried.

Success might have, not success from a single job, but success that arose as a groundswell of support—as it had in the first decades. But after those first decades he never had that, and in the '30's he seems continually bothered by the "bloodshed," as if the uphill climb was too severe. He seemed continually plagued even though he quickly grew happy—"have had many bouquets"—over each individual success. Each was temporary, never stretching into enough of a continuum to emotionally—and perhaps normally—sustain him.

But his focus with the new '30's was so much of a different angle that he probably could not tell when he was successful. And he never realized quite how good his small-town and rural photographs in the '30's were.

He tried to make his words do as if they were photographs and with a quick flash short-circuit a feeling or slip a word in to snatch up a whole situation. In 1930, in the midst of the Great Depression, he wrote to Paul Kellogg, "Can you spare a quarter (of an hour) some day..." The Empire State Building became "Al's Big Shanty" (Al Smith was its major public sponsor). When the short circuit did not work, the words became sticky and sentimental. He described his work portraits as "Characters of the Cast." Sometimes, a silly—but heartfelt—exuberance spilled all over, as when his son recovered from an accident and Hine reported to *Survey* from "the Clipper Ship Hine disabled by collision (that) we are bouncing along over the bounding Main and many-a-happy-day-will-blow When-Hine-Comes-Home-Again."

Then, as if running away from the opening he had created, he adopted short cuts for others to reach him. He addressed Savel Zimand, a man he barely knew, as "Zim," a name no one else ever called him. He scrawled H from H on the H across his stationery in the '20's (Hine from Hastings-on-the-Hudson) and changed it to Hastening-up-the-Hudson in the '30's. Trying to communicate some quick zest-ridden satisfaction he often signed his letter "T. Hine/L. Hine." At other times,

feeling especially pleased with himself he tried to turn a written word into a picture: "Hine" was followed by an arrow curving out, around and under.

Vain attempts! As if he could find expression in the written word and use language to communicate! In effect these became furtive little darts, his photographic eye picking up quick flairs and connections.

In 1938 the Carnegie Corporation denied him a grant to prepare a permanent folio of his photographs, and though terribly wounded, he wrote to Paul Kellogg that there was "still plenty of fight left in this old hulk." He rather constantly referred to his life as a ship, as if he experienced the rocking and challenging rhythms that unpredictable waters only can produce. In that same year, Beaumont Newhall, then a young art critic, now Director of the George Eastman House, visited Hine after reading of him in an article by Elizabeth McCausland, and wrote of his work then to a new and younger art photography world. It looked as if he might experience some new wave of respect. CBS asked him to prepare a series of broadcasts on the working man—on his idea of life and labor. Soon after, the BBC in London asked him to prepare a similar sort of single broadcast. He was pleased that "a coupla government guys (think) my documentary photography (is) the only work of that kind between Civil War Brady and the present." *Life* bought up some of his "old treasures." Ramona Javitz at the New York Public Library started a group of his works for a permanent collec-

45

tion. Charles Adams in Albany (Hine's old economics teacher at the University of Chicago) set up a permanent exhibition at the New York State Museum. And in 1939 the Russell Sage people commissioned him to prepare two folios of his life's work, one on Child Labor, another on Immigrants. This was the same organization that printed many of Hine's photos in the first and second decades. And a third and fourth folio were being negotiated.

But when he died suddenly two years later there had not been enough to build a new base. The Museum of Modern Art in New York City refused his collection. A *Dictionary of American Biography* article could find only limited place for him, and Ewing Galloway echoed that sentiment, putting his negatives on the inactive shelf. Only after additional years have gone by can one see the regenerative life in his photographs. Perhaps, too, the flat inside fury he provoked comes nearer to a present-day emotional response than it did to earlier emotional styles.

Hine always seemed to need money. In 1921 Hine cashed in an insurance policy, and in 1930 when he wanted to sell his house he needed the money. He photographed schoolchildren for private schools in the '30's, and then, for additional monies, compiled brochures of a school's activities—often for *its* money-raising attempts. When Beaumont Newhall visited Hine in 1938, he thought Hine lived near the poverty line. And Victor Weybright remembers he and Hine sometimes spoke of Hine's near-poverty, Hine rather dismissing it with a smile, presuming he could do nothing about it.

How greatly Hine needed seemed always to be balanced by a pressing professional concern. "Need" had to satisfy his professional image of himself. For major jobs he set his fees high. Whether he collected or not after that initial agreement may not have mattered as much as the approval inherent in the high fee. The other's commitment became an expression of his value. Nothing humble or pure. High fees represented excellent work. One government agency refused to hire him because "we could get photographs of the drought taken more cheaply by State Employment Relief Administration." The TVA allotted him $1,075 for an initial survey, salary at the rate of $500 per month. This in 1933, as Depression wages otherwise sank. But to his friends at *Survey* in the 1930's he often sold an old photograph for a $5.00 reproduction fee, refused to take *Survey* money for the TVA shots because he had been paid for them already. And of his $1,075 TVA budget, he only used $615, drawing only a half month's salary for the last part of October he spent there. He needed the expression of value, not the money.

... Needed, that is, for his restless private world protected him more thickly as the years moved on. Where he had found place for his restless biting energies in the widening thrust of the first decade's expectations, where his conscious commitment had pushed his private world out into the great multitude of the early decades, by the end of the '30's his private world was encased and separated. Earlier they harmonized and he still thought they could. In a publicity statement he prepared in 1938 he said, "Work itself has ever been one of the deepest satisfactions that come to the restless human soul." As if reflecting upon the century's span of near forty years he felt the fruition out of work in the city would most satisfy his and any human's restless soul. But it didn't cradle his in the '30's, and his own conscious and unconscious harmonized only when he focused on a natural wooded setting. And that did not fit the '30's pattern he lived with.

By 1939, "needed" took on a different meaning. In September of 1939 the Home Owners Loan Corporation threatened to foreclose his home and Hine seems both terribly upset and accepting of it. He mentions it to Paul Kellogg. And after a series of letters in which he establishes that he does not have either the money or the expectations of a regular—albeit low—income upon which to build a system of payments, he writes a last letter to the agency assuring them he has acted in good faith. More than the house he wanted their knowledge that he did not have the money to shape a system of payments. From January 1st, 1940, he paid rent for his house.

One month before the need for money became desperate as a stable part of his life was endangered. Mrs. Hine was hospitalized and he writes to *Survey* for money, to *Russell Sage* for advanced payment, to *Russell Sage* again to urge them to adopt a third and fourth folio. Wherever a financial arrangement existed he tried to draw out the money quickly. And on Christmas Day 1939, Sara Rich Hine died of pneumonia. Hine never seemed to have recovered and in the following November he died.

Hine shaped a new art form. Not photography. Steiglitz and the Photo-Secessionists did that in this country. But a kind of photography he called "interpretive," later schools called documentary, a base from which the F64 people in San Francisco and the Bauhaus group in Germany grew in the '20's: a flat fiery arrangement of people, light, and form that became a timeless humanist art. The particular situations Hine saw are gone. The splintery wood posts and picket fences and pinpointed array of pebbles are all gone. Even the overt horror he wanted to communicate is gone. But overtly furious with the evils of modern life, he roamed around behind them and saw only the particular people and how they felt about their situation. Even in the '30's as he rested in the comfort of small-town and rural America he saw, probably unbeknownst even to himself, only the particularities—particular people, shapes, lines, and movement. Hine was often described as easy-going. He moved slowly and if we watched him for long, he would look familiar and

47

floppy, probably inefficient, and maybe even inef-fectual. He shaped people as they saw their experi-ences, as if they had most perfectly abstracted crucial conflicts from their lives. In a way Hine did not in-terpret at all. He just came closer and closer to that humanist essence that binds truth and beauty together.

What Hine's eye saw, Hine never wrote about. He wrote empathetically, voiced a disgust, raised hopes, dreamed. He felt the shame of hearing Olga's mother call her "ugly" because she cried when she came home after picking shrimp from 5:00 a.m. on. Olga was eight. He thought that work portraits would present the "human side of industry." And he fondly called the Empire State builders "Skyboys." He identified the blameworthy, idolized the honorary, quipped about the marvelous; and even talked endlessly about them. But he always wrote and talked around the photograph, never directly of it. His eye abstracted and the photo-graph spoke for itself.

48   Hine truly believed he could order a Ruskin-esque life in the city, that his age could transplant natural growth to the city and from the smoke stacks see hu-man fruition rise. Somewhat disgusted—probably an-grily disgusted by 1914 when nothing seemed to be changing, he raised his hopes in 1920. And in 1938, two years before he died, he still advertised his work as showing the "true dignity and integrity of labor"—all labor. To come closer and closer upon that word "true," to search out "dignity" and explore how "work

itself has ever been one of the deepest satisfactions" in this new industrial society: this was Hine's life.

By pursuing that transmutation Hine created a new art form. Both Andre Malraux as critic and Ben Shahn as painter talk of a new art form arising from the artist's inability to communicate within the old. When no form exists through which the artist can funnel his creation or impose his desire he breaks out of those containments to create new ones. In 1911 and again in 1915 Sidney Allen, an art and photography critic, spoke of the need to break away from the old for-malities, from the diffuse light the Photo-Secessionists had made popular. Hine could not tell his audience then nor even tell us now of the many-faceted natural expectations he saw in the city. He knew words failed him and resignedly "lugged" his camera instead. He could talk about evils and dreams and glories and he did tell us the names, ages, and mills. But he could not talk about Mary's dreams. And he could not even photograph Mary's dreams and expectations until he broke out of Impressionism's softly diffused light. He could not explain the "almost" quality of the girl bring-ing the home-worked flowers back to the factory and could only photograph it when he posed the front face of the man in lower left, used the door for a plane, partly covered the girl's face, and relieved and created intensity through light and shadow and a clear linear definition. Hine's passions and thoughts, no matter how personal, were far too intense to sit quietly within traditional vanishing points and frosty lighting. Hine had to re-define and re-balance groups, re-direct light and re-light interiors, re-set the vanishing point and juxtapose movement within the many planes crushing in upon the people he photographed.

In so many Hine photographs one finds movement threatening to spill over and force its way out of the plane that encompasses it. Was his photography the parallel to the "Naturalist" literary school? Too bad the editions of Dreiser of this period use filmy stylized illustrations. But like Sidney Allen who asked for a new style when Hine had already created it, developments that are contemporaneous with each other are often unrecognizable by their creators. A whole new imminence is created by Hine compositions. What he does not say explicitly even while using clear direct lines, what he suggests even while "detective" work pushed him, what he implies even while exposing, becomes the basis of the new art form.

Design always challenges formlessness whether it is human design challenging human formlessness or pictorial design challenging pictorial formlessness. Between the lack of form and the presence of form an inherent conflict looms—then clashes. Lumpen formlessness will not stay that way. The desire for order prods that formlessness. Whether design is shaped out of human purpose as Hine did, out of urban still life as Edward Hopper did, or out of Nature's wealth as Ansel Adams does today—commitment pushes and

speeds that formlessness into some shape. Force the rampant run of movement. Tighten that movement with design. Thrust light at an unexpected subject, re-cast planes, counterbalance lines against people, and the counterpointed rhythms can only explode. Conflict within art increases the communication.

Overt passion destroys that conflict; secreted passion heightens it. Hine secreted passion.

Hine sat within the formlessness of the first decades. Pieces, separated one from another, milled about. People, organizations, expectation, and sheer footloose growth clashed and moved and produced still further alacrity and friction and still further independent and self-directed growth. Hine shaped much of that aimless wandering formlessness into history. He found the conflicts and posed the realities. But his great genius came as he pin-pointed some of that rolling inundating mass of activity into perfected humanist statements. Catching the convergence of an artistic compositional conflict at exactly the same point he found a particularly intense human conflict, he narrowed the gap between conflicting players. Between the rolling formlessness on the one hand and the expectation to be shaped out of it on the other—out of that arena of conflict and the continuous attempts to make that gap tangible, Hine's art springs. We want to narrow that gap so much that we will change its "almost" to a fact, and make that pervasive imminence real. Expectation and imminence, both flowing out of

49

conflict, emerge from a Hine photograph. Possibility and future—dreams germane to both art and history—are still read with a Hine photo.

Hine was cremated on November 4, 1940, a day after he died, with some few friends gathered about him. Eight years earlier, Charles F. Weller, who had known Hine since 1906 when Hine helped him photograph Negro slums in Washington, D.C. wrote to Hine that he was "proud . . . and grateful" for Hine's work—"grateful," he continued, "for your patient, plodding, courageous soaring genius." Each word peeled off a layer of Hine; but no sweeping movement even after his death spiralled him into acclaim. Just a mild upsurge; the Pittsburgh *Bulletin Index* wanted a few select prints, a Boston library created a permanent collection, a Hollywood movie maker wanted others. Certainly not enough to thrust him or his work into the limelight. Yet his work never vanished.

In recent years, curiously enough, more and more Hine photographs appear and re-appear—as if surfacing from some insistent background undercurrent. Hine photographs illustrate TV specials. Labor union advertisements use them—to sentimentalize the past and usually with no credit to Hine—but use them. So, too, with book illustrations and magazine articles. *Life* used a double spread of Hine photographs when it celebrated the 50th anniversary of the founding of the NCLC in 1954—identified him in the text but never indexed his name. And most recently Marshall McLuhan's *The Medium is the Massage* used a Hine photograph without credit or reference—or probably the knowledge that it was a Hine photograph. Up to now, his images have been too far removed from the present, even too far removed from the imminent sense of revelation one needs to be gripped by a work of art. They've been in the background—just the "old favorites" as he called them—and one has stumbled on them. Now our years are catching up with his vision. While his images slid onto a sort of national subliminal shelf and became a part of our national conscience, the eyes of his subjects continued to haunt us—almost insidiously. That his own "restless human soul" outgrew its origins, that it burst all the conventional bounds of photographic inspiration and practice, even that it soared into genius, Hine wished for but probably never fully understood had happened. We are just beginning to realize its relevance and see what it saw.

Selected Bibliography

I. CAMERA TECHNIQUE

Hine used a 5 x 7 view camera, magnesium powder for night flashes, a rapid rectilinear lens, and glass plates when he started photographing in 1903. During World War I he used film and glass plates, the film 4 x 5, the glass plates both 4 x 5 and 5 x 7. His Empire State series was the first major series he did with safety film—all 4 x 5. By 1920 he seemed to have turned exclusively to a 4 x 5 graflex and for the rest of his life worked out an adapter for it using either an eight or five inch lens, giving him medium long and medium short focus. He rarely used filters.

II. COLLECTIONS

A. The George Eastman House holds the best single survey of Hine's life and work. It contains all that was in Hine's house at the time of his death. It contains four loosely packed boxes of mss. material: letters, notes, ideas, statements, scraps, appointments—for the most part remnants of a man's life. In addition, there are about four thousand film and glass negatives covering a few of his treasured favorites, his personal record of France, most of his dreary commercial '20's and '30's work—the Montclair Library, the Hastings School graduation, etc.—and samples from each period of his life. More than four-fifths of the negatives come from 1919 on.

The original prints collection creates a slightly different image than do the negatives. The array is not as vast. But they do seem to represent more fully what he considered to be his best. He blew up some of these "old favorites" and printed others in a sepia tone. Most of them (perhaps 90%) are 8″ x 10″ black and whites. This collection came to the George Eastman House through the Photo League, Corydon Hine, son of Lewis Hine, having given it to the Photo League after Hine died. The Photo League tried to make contact prints of all the negatives but never did. The George Eastman House set itself the same goal but has not finished.

There are about 4,000 negatives; approximately 2,000 contact prints; and about 2,000 original prints. About 350 prints, culled from each of these sources, are filed for ordering purposes.

B. The Library of Congress contains two separate groups of Hine material. One is catalogued. The other becomes a group only after one has gone through the total American Red Cross Collection and finds the Hine material. The catalogued group, the work Hine did for the National Child Labor Committee, comes to 5,000 original prints (with only about 100 matching negatives); a catalogued caption file runs with it. The American Red Cross Collection contains 60,000 photographs taken of Red Cross activities up to 1930, and was given to the Library of Congress in 1944. The American Red Cross had started cataloguing each photograph by subject and place—not by photographer. The Library of Congress has reassigned numbers but not catalogued those numbers nor identified the photographs. The photographer's name usually does not appear either on the caption or on the file card. Close to 1,000 Hine negatives and prints are spread through this collection. One must locate them from other internal and external evidence. They cover his World War I experiences and some of his West Virginia and Arkansas drought experiences.

C. All the work Hine did for the American Red Cross since 1930 is at the American Red Cross headquarters—once again, not indexed to Hine but just the time and place of the photograph. Except for one or two that the American Red Cross used in some of its major publicity drives, they are in inactive files. Primarily negatives, they number about

500, and like the American Red Cross photographs in the Library of Congress must be found through other evidence.

D. The Prints and Photographs Division of the National Archives maintains the photographic record that Hine left as Chief Photographer for the National Research Project on Reemployment Opportunities for the Works Progress Administration. They are photographs primarily of industrial areas in New England and the middle states with a complete caption file. The collection is dotted with some of his earlier industrial and child labor photographs. Just positives; about 500.

E. The University of Minnesota Social Welfare History Archives Center acquired the *Survey* magazine correspondence file from approximately 1920 on; and as a by-product, presumably received fifty prints (no negatives) that happened to be in those files at the time of the gift. They cover Hine's small-town and rural concerns of the '30's.

F. The Tennessee Valley Authority Graphics Department keeps a clear complete collection of the negatives, positives, and captions Hine did for the TVA in October of 1933. There are close to 150.

G. The National Committee on the Employment For Youth keeps approximately the same 5000 prints the Library of Congress has. Though it has no negatives and keeps no separate caption file, some prints are captioned on the back.

H. Approximately 350 positives of the 1,000 Empire State exposures are in the Avery Library of the Columbia University School of Architecture, all a part of the recently acquired Empire State Collection. All are Hine's original prints and about 250 of them match negatives in the George Eastman House. None of the collection, including the Hine material, is filed or catalogued.

I. Hine gave approximately 50 positives to the Picture Service Collection at the New York Public Library in the '30's, gathering one or two exposures from each of many phases of his life into this group. Most are the predictable "old favorites."

J. The Hine Collection in the Local History and Genealogy Division Room of the New York Public Library contains the most perfect positives Hine ever made of his own work. Printed in 1939 and 1940, he prepared these for the Russell Sage Foundation when he was commissioned to prepare a documentation of his work. Two units, one on child labor and another on Immigrants, make up the approximate 250 photographs. The miscellaneous folder suggests the moment when he died, for approval was pending on two more units.

K. About 125 Hine negatives (all in the inactive file) are at Ewing Galloway. Hine selected these in the '30's from his past. A few came out of his personal work.

L. Some private collections are spotted about, all, for the most part, small and generally insignificant. The Community Service Society, for instance, has some Hine photographs stretched through the scrapbooks they acquired from their parent organizations—the Charity Organization Society and the Association for the Improvement of the Condition of the Poor, for both of which it seems Hine worked in 1905, 1906, and 1907. They have about 350 photographs of which there may be 50 Hine's. The International Ladies Garment Workers Union has a few dozen. The Amalgamated Clothing Workers keeps a similarly small number. The Ethical Culture Schools located some brochure photographs. Individuals throughout the New York City area own a few Hine photographs . . . as for instance does Andre Blumenthal the son of the Sydney Blumenthal who operated Shelton Looms, photographers like Berenice Abbott and Elizabeth McCausland, etc. Every so often Hine would give a friend one of his favorites, especially as it seemed clearer and clearer to him that the triumph he expected might never come. He might at least experience a contentment—maybe a glory—from amongst his friends.

Hine did work for one of the recreational associations that has since merged into the National Recreation and Park Association. The mss. of the National Recreation Association, the association preceding the final amalgamation, are now at the Social Welfare History Archives Center in Minneapolis. My guess is that an assortment of uncatalogued Hine photographs are there.

And at some point more of the Empire State photographs may well turn up.

III. FIRST PUBLISHED HINE PHOTOGRAPHS

The following are references to photographs, not articles. Even though more than half of the following photographs exist in a story either written by Hine or developed predominantly out of his photographs, I have used the photograph as the guide and not the written word or indexed feature. Hine was a photographer.

A. Magazines
The Charities and Commons

Vol. 20: June 5—cover "Ellis Island Girl"; Aug. 1—cover "Kids Shooting Crap"; Sept. 5—pp 644 *ff* "As They Come to Ellis Island".

Vol. 21: Dec. 5, 1908—cover; Jan. 2, 1909—pp 580 *ff* "Immigrant Types In The Steel District"; pp 613-628 "Homestead"; Jan. 30—pp 742 *ff* "Child Labor In The Carolinas"; Feb. 6—pp 913-920 "The Mill Town Courts and Their Lodgers"; Mar. 6—pp 1054-1059 "Wage Earners of Pittsburgh"; pp 1116-1126 "The Industrial Environment of Pittsburgh's Working Women".

The Charities and Commons continues as *Survey*

Vol. 22: Apr. 3—pp 111 *ff* "Climbing Into America"; May 1—pp 196 *ff* "The Irregularity of Employment of Women Factory Workers"; July 3—pp 488 *ff* "The Way of the Girl".

Vol. 23: Oct. 2, 1909—"Southerners of Tomorrow"; Jan. 1, 1910—16 pp insert & pp 449 *ff* "Construction Camps of the People"; pp 481 *ff* "Roving Children".

Vol. 24: Apr. 2—p 18 "Backyards and Alleys in South Chicago"; p 21 "The Steel Mill Fence"; Apr. 16—cover "Delivering Easter Bonnets"; pp 105 *ff* "How Girls Learn the Millinery Trade"; Apr. 23—cover "South Side Chicago"; Apr. 30—p 187 letter from Hine; May 28—cover "In the Babies Ward"; July 2—pp 548 *ff* "City Neighbors at Play"; July 30—cover "Neighbor at Hull House"; Aug. 6—p 672 "Bohemian Woman on Ellis Island"; Aug. 20—cover "One of the New New Englanders"; Aug. 27—cover "The Next Generation: Charleston"; Sept. 10—cover "Southern Cotton Mill Boy"; Sept. 24—cover "Life in Harlem is a Serious Business".

Vol. 25: Jan. 7—pp 570-578 *ff* "Findings of the Immigration Commission"; pp 605 *ff* "Cost of Cranberry Sauce"; Jan. 14—p 644; Feb. 4—pp 768 *ff* "Housing Awakening"; Feb. 4—pp 772-781 "Homework in the Tenements".

Vol. 26: Apr. 8—p 86 "Millinery Shop" reprints.

Vol. 27: Dec. 2, 1911—pp 1286 *ff* "Bethlehem"; p. 1275 "Newsboy"; Jan. 6, 1912—pp 1520 *ff* "Conservation of Childhood".

Vol. 28: Apr. 6—pp 8 *ff*, p 17; June 29—cover "Girl from Mill"; Aug. 24—cover "Hull House Women"; Aug. 31—cover "Yarn Inspector"; Sept. 14—cover "Father Neptune".

Vol. 29: Oct. 5, 1912—pp 6 *ff* "Old Mill Hand Young Steel Worker"; Oct. 26—p 109 ad; Nov. 2—cover "Girl on Playground"; Dec. 28—pp 392 *ff* NCLC ads; Jan. 4, 1913—cover "Box Factory Worker".

Vol. 30: May 3—pp 167-177 "Baltimore to Biloxi and Back".

Vol. 31: Oct. 4, 1913—inside cover Hine ad; Oct. 18—inside cover same ad; Oct. 25—inside cover same ad; Nov. 22—cover "Girl in Cranberry Bogs"; Dec. 6—cover "Mother and Child"; p 245 "Mother and Child"; Jan. 17, 1914—p 455 "Newsboy" photo; (Dec. 20 journal ad. and Jan. 10 journal ad. use Hine photos); Jan. 24—p 500 "Flowers of the Tenement Child"; Feb. 7—cover "5-year-old Cotton Picker"; p 583 "Home Hospital Experiment"; pp 589 *ff* "Children or Cotton"; Feb. 14—p 632 ad using photo; Feb. 21—p 637 Time Exposure by Hine: "School Opens at 6:00"; Feb. 28—p 663 Time Exposure by Hine: "Cannery"; Mar. 7—p 691 Time Exposure: "Hiding Behind Work Certificate"; Mar. 14 p 737 Time Exposure: "Girl Worker in a Cotton Mill"; Mar. 21—p 765 Time Exposure: "Not a Vacation Farm; Just a Maryland Cannery".

Vol. 32: Apr. 4—p 5 Time Exposure by Hine: "Double Standard"; Apr. 11—p 49 poster with Hine photo; Apr. 18—p 69 Time Exposures: "Illiterates in Massachusetts"; Apr. 18—pp 80 *ff* "Boyhood and Lawlessness on the West Side of New York"; May 9—back cover "Opening the Canal"; ad.; p 171 Time Exposures by Hine: "Cotton Picking"; May 16—p 192 Time Exposures: "Cans and Kids"; May 23—p 212 Time Exposures: "Outside the Poor Mans Club"; June 20—ad; July 4—p 382 ad; July 11—p 388 Time Exposures: "Chicago Sin and Brothel"; Aug. 1—p 446

Time Exposures: "Kids on City Streets"; Aug. 8—p 475 "Boy"; Aug. 22—p 517 "The Girls They Leave Behind Them"; Aug. 29—facing p 535 ad; Sept. 5—p 556 Time Exposures: "In the Cool of the Evening"; inside cover ad.

Vol. 33: Oct. 3, 1914—p 36 ad; Nov. 7—p 161 ad; Dec. 5—p 226 ad; p 275 *Pittsburgh Survey* ad uses Hine photo; Dec. 19—p 325 ad; Jan. 2, 1915—back cover ad; Feb. 20—p 553 Time Exposures: "Cigar Reader"; Feb. 27—p 573 "Child Workers in North Carolina Cotton Mills"; Mar. 6—ad.

Vol. 34: May 1—p 115 "Immigrants"; May 8—p 134 "Two Little Brothers"; Aug. 21—cover "Vacation Time Never Comes in the School of a City Street".

Vol. 35: Nov. 13, 1915—cover "Hassan Ben Ali"; pp 164 *ff* "Entertainment on Joy Zone in San Francisco Exposition"; Jan. 29, 1916—cover "War Time"; Mar. 4—pp 655 *ff* "Beeters".

Vol. 36: July 1—p 374 "June in the Beet Fields".

Vol. 37: Oct. 14—p 39 "October in the Beet Fields"; Nov. 25—p 203 "November in the Beet Fields"; Dec. 9—p 269 "Night Breadline at the Bowery Mission".

Vol. 38: Apr. 28—p 86 "A Plan to Safeguard Children in Farm Work"; June 6—pp 396 *ff* "Beyond the Reach of the Law"; June 20—p 463 "Out to Win".

Vol. 39: Oct. 27—pp 92 *ff* "Army Camp".

Vol. 40: Aug. 10—cover "Old Age and Youth of France".

Vol. 41: Oct. 12—pp 38 *ff* "St. Etienne"; Nov. 9—p 149 "Negro Head".

Vol. 42: May 31—p 373 "Refugees and Turkish Quarter"; July 5—pp 523-528 "Pull of the Home Tide"; Aug. 2—pp 661-665 "They Departed Into Their Own Country"; Sept. 6—cover; pp 813-817 "Child's Burden in the Balkans".

Vol. 43: Oct. 4—p 19 "Empty"; Nov. 8—pp 79-83 "The War and Children".

Vol. 45: Jan. 15—p 559 "Child Labor Day". (With Volume 47, *Survey* issued a graphic number once a month. The October 29, 1921, issue was the first.)

Vol. 47: Oct. 29, 1921—pp 159-166 "The Railroaders"; Dec. 31—pp 511-518 "Power Makers"; Feb. 25, 1922—pp 851-858 "Harbor Workers"; Mar. 25—pp 991 *ff* "Coal Portraits"; p 1005 "Coal in West Virginia"; pp 1014 *ff* "In the Mines".

Vol. 48: July 1—pp 455-462 "Hine Postal Workers"; Sept. 1—cover; pp 669-676 "Truck Workers".

Vol. 49: Feb. 1—cover "Joy in Work" (Printer).

Vol. 51: Oct. 1, 1923—p 4 "Negro Woman and Baby"; Nov. 1—p 155 "The Homes of the Free"; Jan. 1, 1924—p 310 "A Railroad Shop Man"; Feb. 1—pp 456-464A "Medieval Industry in the 20th Century" (Hatmakers); Mar. 1—pp 595-599 "Giant Power Makers"; pp 595, 629, 632 "Tools of the Trade—Powerhouse Workers".

Vol. 52: July 1—p 419 "Portrait of Arthur Gleason"; Sept. 1—pp 571-575 "Going to School in a Textile Mill".

Vol. 53: Nov., 1924—pp 119 *ff*, pp 126 *ff*, p 133 (all on Heart Disease); Jan., 1925—pp 383-389 Camera Studies by Hine on Rural Health and Child Labor.

Vol. 55: Nov.—p 120 "Can We Survive in Crowds in Cities?"; pp 129-133 "Guardians of City Health".

Vol. 56: Apr.—pp 15-17 "Doomsday for Diphtheria".

Vol. 62: Apr. 1—p 54 "Portraits of Amalgamated Clothing Workers"; Aug. 1—pp 473 *ff* "Good Scouts".

Vol. 63: Dec. 1, 1929—pp 261-264 "Styles in Strikes"; p 282 "Shepherdess Knitting"; Jan. 1, 1930—p 438 ad.

Vol. 64: May 1—pp 120-123 "Straightening Young Twigs".

Vol. 65: Jan. 1—pp 361 *ff* "From the City Streets".

Vol. 67: Mar. 1—pp 578 *ff* "Where Precision Begins".

Vol. 68: June 1—cover "Girl at Walden"; p 351 "Warden Brown".

Survey Graphic—Starting with this volume, the graphic number became a more distinct magazine with a separate name and different subscribers.

Vol. 22: Apr.—pp 210-211 "Through the Threads"; Sept.—p 446 "A 14-year old in Mule Room".

Vol. 23: Jan.—p 4 "Young Farmer Becomes Sawyer"; pp 6 & 7 "Construction View"; pp 9 & 10 all TVA area; Mar.—p 106 More TVA area; Aug.—p 389 "Montclair, New Jersey Library"; Sept.—pp 421-427 "Man Off the Road"; p 435 portrait of Arthur Kellogg; Nov.—pp 549 ff "Bench Marks in the Tennessee Valley" (uncredited); Dec.—pp 608-609 "Here We Are".

Vol. 24: Mar.—pp 112-115 "The Man on the Job" Hine's TVA (uncredited); June—pp 289-292 "Park Benches and Park Projects".

Vol. 25: Dec.—p 670 "Rural America".

Vol. 26: Jan.—pp 10 & 11 "Children Wanted"; May—pp 275-279 "Manpower, Skills Change"; Dec.—pp 639-642 "Work Portraits".

Vol. 27: Oct.—p 484 "Worker"; pp 502-505 "Portrait of a Photographer".

Vol. 28: Jan.—pp 13-17 "Americans Ship Out"; p 20 portrait of Joe Curran; Oct.—p 604 "Crossroads School" (a Hine photo credited to FSA).

Vol. 29: Dec.—p 614 obit.

Craftsman—Vol. 13: Jan. 1908—pp 400-408 "Industrial Training for Deaf Mutes".

Education—Vol. 29: Oct. 1908—pp 84-91 "Question of the School Excursion".

Elementary School Teacher—Vol. 6: Mar. 1906—pp 343-347 "School Camera".

Everybody's
Vol. 18: Dec.—pp 798 ff "The Woman's Invasion" by Emmet V. O'Neill and Lewis W. Hine.
Vol. 21: July—pp 75-87 "Unto the Least of These".
Vol. 27: Nov.—pp 536-543 "At the Bottom".
Vol. 29: Aug.—pp 246-255 "Big Brothers and Little".
Vol. 39: July—pp 66 & 67 "Play Time at the Training Camps"; Sept.—pp 40 & 41 "The Stuff That Makes Our Fighting Force"; Oct.—pp 52 & 53 "The Yankee Stew".

Fortune—Vol. 192: June—pp 78-91 "A Railroad Fireman".

McClure's—Vol. 35: July—pp 231-240 "Toilers of the Tenements"; Oct.—pp 595-607 "Working Girls' Budgets".

Outlook
Vol. 83: July 28—pp 712-719 "Schools in the Park".
Vol. 84: Oct. 27—pp 502-506 "Indian Summer".
Vol. 93: Sept. 25—pp 153-159 "The Social Engineer in Pittsburgh"; Oct. 23—pp 435-443 "Day Labourers Before Their Time".
Vol. 116: June 6—pp 224-227 "The American Gamin".

Photographic Times
Vol. 38: Nov.—pp 488-490 "The Silhouette in Photography".
Vol. 40: Aug.—pp 227-232 "Photography in the School".

U.S. Camera Annual—1941—p 77 "Railroad Cabman"; 1942—p 58 "Railroad Engineer".

World Today—Vol. 13: Dec. 1907—pp 1254-1258 "Charity on a Business Basis".

World's Work
Vol. 38: Oct.—pp 641-648 "Peace-Time Pioneers".
Vol. 60: Mar.—p 77 "The Steel Aviators".

B. NATIONAL CHILD LABOR COMMITTEE PAMPHLETS

All of these pamphlets grew out of Hine's photographs. Some were written—as was the material often investigated—solely by Hine; some were co-authored by Hine; some were "illustrated" by Hine. All came from material he and/or others prepared as a report for the National Child Labor Committee.

The National Child Labor Committee put out both pamphlets and bulletins. The pamphlet usually cost five or ten cents, used a number to identify it and represented a more long standing issue. A bulletin, on the other hand, often came out first, was identified by a month and date and became the basis for later-issued pamphlets. The material's first public airing, though, usually came at any one of the National Child Labor Committee's annual conferences. Original, blown-up, or stereopticon versions of the photographs were presented. Hine often addressed the conference and the address(es) and some of the photographs usually appeared in the report of the conference and/or as the Proceedings of the Conference. Independent of these organizationally issued statements, the material often appeared—often with the same or adapted wording—as an article in any one of the muckraking or reform journals of the period.

NCLC Pamphlets
Child Labor in West Virginia, Ed N. Clopper, #86
Child Labor in the Carolinas, #92
Child Labor in the Gulf Coast Canneries, L. W. Hine, #158
The Child's Burden in the Canneries, #193
People Who Go to Tomatoes, Harry Bremer, #215
Child Labor Selections for Audiences' use for Children's Day or Special Children's Meetings, #220
Child Work in The Home, Jessie P. Rich and Lewis W. Hine, #232 ("Tasks in the Tenements" is a sub-unit of this)
The High Cost of Child Labor, #241
Vocational Guidance and Child Labor, #244
Street Workers, #246
Child Labor in the Sugar Beet Fields of Colorado, #259
The Child in the Cotton Mill, #260
Organized Labor and Child Labor Reform, #261
The Citizen and the NCLC, #266
More Education Pays, #270
Farmwork and Schools in Kentucky, #274
Children in Agriculture, #284
Children Who Work in Our Streets, #294
Children in Strawberries, #380
Leaves of Absence From Rural Schools in Oklahoma, #381

NCLC Bulletins
Poverty and Child Labor.
Child Labor in Georgia. July 12, 1910.
Child's Burden in Oyster and Shrimp Canneries. May 1913.
Little Comrades Who Toil. Aug. 1914.
Can We Afford Child Labor? Feb. 1915.
Child Labor Facts. 1939-40.

Child Workers in Tenements.
Children on Stage.

C. BOOKS (only those with first published Hine photos)
Street-Land Its Little People and Big Problems, Philip Davis assisted by Grace Kroll. Small, Maynard, and Company Inc. Boston 1915.
Rural Child Welfare, NCLC under direction of Ed Clopper. Macmillan. New York 1922.
Boyhood and Lawlessness, one volume in the series, *West Side Studies,* under the direction of Pauline Goldmark. Russell Sage Foundation.
The Pittsburgh Survey ed. Paul Underwood Kellogg. Charities Publication Committee.
Vol. 1. *The Pittsburgh District Symposium,* John R. Commons, Robert A. Woods, Florence Kelley, Charles Mulford Robinson and others.
Vol. 2. *The Steel Workers,* John A. Fitch.
Vol. 3. *Homestead: The Households of a Steel Town,* Margaret F. Byington.
Vol. 4. *Women and the Trades,* Elizabeth Beardley Butler.
Vol. 5. *Work Accidents and the Law,* Crystal Eastman.
Vol. 6. *Pittsburgh: The Gist of the Survey,* Paul U. Kellogg.
Neglected Neighbors in the National Capital, Charles F. Weller, The John C. Wonston Co., Philadelphia, 1909.
A Seasonal Industry (a study of the Millinery Trade in New York), Mary Van Kleeck. Russell Sage Foundation, 1917.
Empire State. A history. Pub. by Empire State Inc. 1931.

D. BROCHURES, etc.
Hine photographs appeared in various publicity and advertising media. Sloan's liniments ads in the late 20's used some of his portraits of working men to illustrate the triumph men achieve in their work. Tiffany's apparently used some of his craftsmen. Printing companies used his printer. "Empire Statements," a publicity advertising brochure distributed by the Empire State Corporation to induce renters to take space in the new building used his Empire State photographs. The NCLC bulletins published ads for *Survey Magazine* using his photos just as *Survey* received ads from NCLC with his photographs. Ethical

Culture and Walden schools used his photographs to publicize their schools in brochures, and the Shelton Looms used his photographs in publicity brochures as well as in blow-ups at the industrial exhibit they maintained at Chicago World's Fair in 1933. Correspondence points to J. Walter Thompson's pirated use of his materials in the 20's. Some of his Bellevue Hospital photos were used by others. Government folders apparently used his Research on Manpower shots for the W.P.A. Tracking the photographs became like clearing through drifts—and then coming upon a vast untouched area.

IV. REPRINTS OF HINE PHOTOGRAPHS
It is almost impossible to read through any form of American literature, history, or commentary from the 20th Century without stumbling over Hine photographs. Sometimes they are precisely identified as Hine photographs, sometimes merely identified as a product of a picture service corporation; sometimes they are even laid in without much awareness of their source. Such substantive works as Rexford Guy Tugwell's account of *American Economic Life* in the 30's uses Hine photographs, such overtly passionate statements as Louis Adamic's *From Many Lands* used Hine photographs, such traditional and early sociological accounts as E. A. Ross' *The Old World in the New* used Hine . . . just as the moody modish *au courant The Medium Is the Massage* uses a Hine photograph. So, too with magazines. *The American Child* continually reprinted. *Life* did. *Look* did. Current ads do. To track the path a man's art took as he fell out of the mainstream while his photographs sat on a plateau is an impossible task: they are all over the place, most of them unidentified. Perhaps one of the poignant moments in research for this book came in seeing a set of galleys in Hine's mss. collection with two Hine photos printed on the galleys, a credit to Brown Brothers—and not a comment from Hine although he had written something else along the margin. That was in 1936.

V. MANUSCRIPTS
These became the major sources of information. The correspondence he maintained with Paul Kellogg is at the *Social Welfare History Archives Center* at the University of Minnesota. *George Eastman House* keeps what happened to have been left with Hine at the time of his death. Barely a letter; but scraps and notes and appointments and catalogues and so much of the miscellaneous bits of a person's life that make sense once a pattern emerges. At the *Russell Sage Foundation* correspondence remains from the end portions of his life. Individual letters to a variety and assortment of people whom I tied to Hine because of similar activities at the same time and place in life produced fascinating results. The *American Red Cross* summoned what it could from archives, as did TVA and *National Archives*. In addition, I consulted the papers of Elizabeth McCausland at the *Archives of American Art,* the papers of Homer Folks at the Columbia School of Social Work; the papers of Bell Israels Moscowitz at Connecticut College produce droplets . . . as did the records of the Community Service Society . . . as did the papers of the Empire State Corporation . . . as did the papers of Mabel Boardman at the Library of Congress. I went to the NCLC papers at the Library of Congress expecting much, but barely a letter rests in those papers; just scrapbooks and reports. They played a role in helping to create an understanding of the period, but missed focusing on Hine himself.

VI. ARTICLES
Many articles and newspaper accounts have referred to Hine and indicated his work; but the following deal with Hine critically, many pointing to his role in creating a new form of photography.
"Workers Relation to Industry Shown in Photographic Survey" *New York Post,* October 28, 1920.
"Treating Labor Artistically," *Literary Digest,* Vol. 67, December 4, pp 32 *ff,* 1920.
"The Photo-Interpreters," *Mentor,* Vol. 14, pp 41-47, 1926.
Brooklyn Eagle, November 1929.
"Through The Threads," Sidney Blumenthal, *American Magazine of Art,* pp 439-442, Aug. 1930.
American Magazine, May 1931.
"Former Oshkonian's Skill With Camera Is Told By Woman Who Once Lived Here." *Oshkosh Daily Northwestern,* May 8, 1931.
"Sky Boys Who Rode the Ball," *Literary Digest,* Vol. 109, pp 30 *ff,* May 23, 1931.
"Men and The Skyscraper," by Hester Jenkins, *The Com-*

mercial Photographer, Vol. VI, pp 634-636, Aug. 1931.

Beaumont Newhall, an article on Hine, *Parnassus,* March 1938.

"A Generation Re-Discovered Through Camera Shots," Elizabeth McCausland, *The Springfield Sunday Union and Republican,* Sept. 11, 1938.

"Portrait of a Photographer," Elizabeth McCausland, *Survey Graphic,* Vol. 27, pp 502-505, Oct. 1938.

"Lewis W. Hine", Beaumont Newhall, *Magazine of Art,* Vol. 31, pp 636-637, Nov. 1938.

"Boswell of Ellis Island," Elizabeth McCausland, *U.S. Camera,* January-February 1939.

"Portrait of Lewis Hine," Robert Marks, *Coronet,* Feb. 1939.

Hartford Courant, Nov. 5, 1939.

Friday, Apr. 26, 1940.

"Early Photographs by Lewis W. Hine," *American Photography,* Vol. 44, pp 35-37, Oct. 1950.

"They Led Child Labor Crusade," *Milwaukee Journal,* Sept. 21, 1966.

VII. OTHERS

Two individuals, Beaumont Newhall and Elizabeth Mc-Causland, both art critics, knew Hine at the end of his life. Finding about Hine through Mr. Newhall meant reading what Mr. Newhall wrote—in *Parnassus,* in his *History of Photography,* in the *Dictionary of American Biography,* and talking with him. Elizabeth McCausland wrote and spoke grandiosely about Hine.

Hine was listed in *Who's Who* from 1920 through 1931, and when dropped in 1932 was unnerved. Each of these sketches were helpful . . . as were those of his many contemporaries also listed. Two written pieces started me on my early searches. Robert Doty's article on Hine for the May 1957 issue of *Image,* and a Master's thesis, filed at the University of Rochester: Rochester, New York.

VIII. ON THE PERIOD

To understand the period out of which Hine grew I used monographic and general accounts of the cultural, social, economic and political development of the first part of the century. The mss. papers I first consulted for information on Hine I stayed with and researched in for an understanding of the period until I was able to string ideas and events together about the dynamic new society these years created. Thus, while the NCLC did not furnish me enough Hine material, it did put me into the middle of one of the era's major reform movements. Where Mabel Boardman's papers did not mention Hine once, they did unveil the movements and correspondence of a figure who moved through and shaped much of another reform movement—one that Hine had also been deeply concerned with. And where I had hoped to find references to Hine in the Homer Folks papers (he was Charity Commissioner of New York State from 1905 until he went abroad for the American Red Cross in World War I) I left the papers impressed with the character of a well-bred somewhat upper class reform leader who knew and admired Hine . . . though his business day never included Hine.

Reading the magazines and journals furnished raw data for the explosive nature of the century's first twelve or fifteen years. Hearing William James discuss the college bred in *McClure's* in February 1908 and the glories of nature in *McClure's* in May of 1905 was as provocative as reading Lincoln Steffens, Ida Tarbell, Willa Cather—all after reading Carl Schurz' reminiscences of the period preceding them. And reading of the development of garden cities in England and the newer industrial cities of the United States provoked an understanding of Ernest Pool's fictionalized hopes and the Westmoreland strikers' dashed hopes. The flux of the period became apparent.

To recapture the photographic movement of the period I consulted the photographic journals. *Photographic Times,* for whom Hine wrote, was especially necessary and helpful. *The Photographic News* aired the conflicts of the period, showing the different modes and styles and groups that began to move across the photographic scene. *Photo Era* provided still another set of more "artistic" details. For an historical perspective of photography's growth, Beaumont Newhall's *History of Photography* (Museum of Modern Art, 1964) and Peter Pollack's *The Picture History Of Photography* (Abrams, New York) most demonstratively helped.

For descriptions of the creative art and how it moves from the creator to the plastic representation itself, André Malraux's *The Voices Of Silence* (Doubleday, 1953) and

Ben Shahn's *The Shape Of Content* (Harvard University Press, 1966) were helpful in communicating a feeling tone for that act. Arthur Koestler's *The Act Of Creation* (Macmillan, 1964) a bit less so. Gyorgy Kepes extended notions and explicitly captured the historic development of plastic representation by showing the development of the creative act through the ages. His *The Visual Arts Today* (Wesleyan University Press, 1960) provided some significant perspectives as did in a lesser way each of the six volumes he edited for Brazillier. But in his *Language Of Vision* (Paul Theobold, 1964) he clearly set forth the top spin of the creative act and followed it from the Renaissance up to the present. More generally I used Herbert Read's expositions on the social aspects of art, Hauser's general 3-volume history of the development of art, and consulted Bernard Berenson's lovely involvement with the process and appreciation of art, watching him expose singularly brilliant and sometimes beguiling facets of artistic development.

Milton Brown's book *American Painting From The Armory Show To The Depression* (Princeton University Press, 1955) provided a rather straightforward and necessary account of the development of painting in the period that somewhat paralleled Hine's growth. And articles in *The New Republic,* the *Magazine Of Art, Literary Digest,* and *International Studio* continuously pointed to the facets newly revealed by the latest trends.

IX. HINE SHOWS AND REVIEWS
Civic Art Club, New York City, Oct. 1920.
National Arts Club, New York City, Nov. 1920.
Woman's Club, Hastings-on-the-Hudson, Dec. 1920.
Yonkers Museum, Yonkers, New York, Apr. 1931.
Riverside Museum, New York City, Jan. 1939.
Des Moines Fine Arts Association Gallery, Des Moines, Iowa, Mar. 1939.

Lewis Hine published his only book, *Men At Work* (Macmillan) in 1932. Many claim this to be a forerunner of the picture-book phenomenon. After its appearance, and after each of his shows, he received critical acclaim in the *New York Post, The Hastings News, The Hastings Press,* the *New York World Telegram,* the *New York Times,* the *New York Sun,* the *Christian Science Monitor* and the *Oshkosh Daily Northwestern.*

Currently the George Eastman House is traveling a small Hine show of 75 prints, appearing in select galleries about the countryside. It too is followed by local critical acclaim. For instance when it appeared in the San Francisco Museum of Art in March of 1967, the *San Francisco Chronicle* reviewed it.

Immigrants

Long Leaf Pine. Georgia. 1909.

61

Young Russian Jewess at Ellis Island. 1905.

Elderly Jewish Immigrant. Ellis Island. 1905.

Climbing Into The Land of Promise. Ellis Island. 1905.

Immigrants Going Down Gangplank. New York. 1905.

On the Bowery. New York City. February 6, 1912.

Old Woman. 1905.

Mrs. Raphael Marengin, New York City. 4:00 p.m., December, 1911.

Children—Mostly Working

Mill running at night. Whitnel Cotton Manufacturing Company.
Whitnel, North Carolina. December, 1908.

Some of the Small Boys Working in Amoskeag Manufacturing Company.
Manchester, New Hampshire. 12:00 noon, May 25, 1909.

Mill. Mississippi. 1911.

70

"Hell's Half Acre". Alabama Mill Settlement. 1910.

71

Noon Hour at Massachusetts Mill. Lindale, Georgia. April 12, 1913.

Exterior of Rear Tenement. New York. November, 1912.

Row of Tenements. 260 to 268 Elizabeth Street, New York City. March, 1912.

73

Indiana Glass Works. 9:00 p.m. August, 1908.

Boys Going to Work in Warren Manufacturing Company. Warren, Rhode Island. 6:00 a.m., June 10, 1909.

A Young Oyster Fisher. Apalachicola, Florida. January, 1909.

A view of the Pennsylvania Breaker. The dust was so dense at times as to obscure
the view. South Pittston, Pennsylvania. January, 1911.

77

Manuel Searels, 175 Coggshall Street. Works in Bennel Mill. New Bedford, Massachusetts. January, 1912.

Leo, 48 inches high, 8 years old, picks up bobbins at 15 cents a day.
Fayetteville, Tennessee. November, 1910.

Coming out of Amoskeag Manufacturing Company. Manchester, New Hampshire. 6:00 p.m., May 24, 1909.

Newsies at Skeeter Branch. St. Louis, Missouri. 11:00 a.m., May 9, 1910.

Seven-Year-Old Tommie Noonan Demonstrating the Advantages of the Ideal
Necktie Form. Pennsylvania Avenue near 13th St., Washington, D.C. April, 1912.

Johnston's Branch Adjoining Saloon. 10th and Cass Street,   83
St. Louis, Missouri. May, 1910.

Glass Blower and Mold Boy. Grafton, West Virginia. October, 1908.

84

A few of the Workers on Night Shift at Cumberland Glass Works.
Bridgeton, New Jersey. November 15, 1909.

Freddie Reed, 14 years old, Hayden Street, been working a few months.
Kibbe's Candy Factory. Springfield, Massachusetts. October, 1910.

Boy 12 Years Old Selling Papers. Hartford, Connecticut. March 6, 1909.

Youngest Girl in Window Has Been Spinning in Royal Mill For One Year.
River Point, Rhode Island. April, 1909.

The McFarland Family. Winona, Mississippi. May 11, 1911.

Dinner Time. Family of Mrs. A. J. Young. Tifton, Georgia. January 22, 1909.

Shuckers in the Varn and Platt Canning Company. Yonges Island. 1913.

92

93

Sixth Street Market. Cincinnati, Ohio. 10:00 p.m., August 22, 1908.

Regular Worker (doffer) in Richmond Spinning Mills. Chattanooga, Tennessee.
December, 1910.

Neil Gallagher, Worked Two Years in Breaker. Leg Crushed Between Cars.
Wilkes Barre, Pennsylvania. November, 1909.

Vance, a trapper boy, 15 years old, has trapped for several years in a West Virginia coal mine. West Virginia. September, 1908.

John Dempsey (looked 11 or 12 years old) who said he helped only on Saturdays, working faithfully in the mule-spinning room. Jackson Mill. Fiskeville, Rhode Island. April, 1909.

Polish Boy Taking Noon Rest in Doffer Box. Quidnick Mill. 1909.

Glass Work Boy, Night Shift. Indiana. August, 1908.

Newsies Shooting Craps Near Post Office. Midnight. Providence, Rhode Island.
November 23, 1912.

Messenger Boy Working for Mackay Telegraph Company. Waco, Texas. September, 1913.

102

Dannie Mercurio, 150 Schottes Alley. Washington, D.C. April, 1912.

Boy Going to Work. Merrimac Mills. Huntsville, Alabama. Noon. November, 1910.

104

Girl Entering the Factory Door, 526 West Broadway, with Artificial Flowers Made at Home. Noon. February 6, 1912.

Two Workers at Bates Manufacturing Company. Lewiston, Maine.
6:00 p.m. April 23, 1909.

106

Little Negro Orphan. Washington, D.C. 1906.

Printer. 1905.

108

SECTION   III

Adults Out of the New Industrial Image

Old Cellar Bakery. Before 1910.

Jewish Peddlar. Chicago. Before 1910.

Man from East Side. New York City. Before 1910.

112

Old-Fashioned Street Sweeper. Circa 1910.   113

114   Negro: Tenement Cellar, Washington, 1908.

The Dependent Widower. Meridian, Mississippi. April, 1911.

116

Negro Man. Atlanta (?) Before 1917.

Old Man Inspecting Yarn.
Rhodes Manufacturing Company.
Lincolntown, North Carolina.
November, 1908.

117

Woman Making Cigars.
Tampa, Florida. Circa 1910.

Mrs. Chassin, 335 E. 3rd Street.
Making Hair Goods. New York City.
February, 1912.

Interior of a Steel Mill. Circa 1910.

118

Slavic Coal Miner in Pittsburgh District. 1910.

Hat Forms. New York City. 1915.

120

Millinery Workers. New York City. 1915.

Europe During and After World War I.

Paris Gamin. France. 1918-19.

Combles. France. April, 1919.

The Wooden Crosses in the Foreground Mark the Graves of Bulgarian Soldiers.
Upon the Hillside Those of Serbians. Nish. December, 1918.

122

Greek Refugees Living Temporarily in the Old Greek Church of St. Mins. Salonika, Greece. December, 1918.

France. April, 1919.

124

Refugees on Top of Box Cars. Shumitza, Serbia. December, 1918.

Belgium. April, 1919.

Street Beggars.
Belgrade, Serbia. December, 1918.

126

An Aged Woman in a Burlap Cave. Salonika, Greece. December, 1918.

128

Refugees Following the Railroad Track on Their Way Back to Greletza, Serbia . December, 1918.

129

A Window in One of the Ruins. Salonika, Greece. December, 1918.

Two Starving Children (note bundle of rags, *right*) in Deserted Out-building. Lescowatz, Serbia.

130

131

Little Girl Standing in Doorway. France. 1918-19.

A Street Beggar. Belgrade, Serbia. December, 1918.

132

Man in Latin Quarter Window. France. 1918.

Paper Woman #1. Bordeaux, France. 1918.

The Red Cross Furnishes Food in Paris. August, 1918.

137

Hine: Caught by the camera. Snapped as he was trying to photograph a crowd of
refugees arriving at the American Red Cross canteen beside the Gare du Nord. Paris, France. June, 1918.

Men and Power

Man at Dynamo. 1921 or 1923.

Rivet Heater. Empire State Building. New York City. 1930-31.

140

Steel Worker. Empire State Building. New York City. 1931.

Empire State Building. New York City. 1930.

Man With Pneumatic Drill. Empire State Building. New York City. 1931.

Steel Worker. Empire State Building. New York City. 1931.

144

Lower New York Design. New York City. 1931.

Avenue of Girders. Empire State Building. New York City. 1930.

Small-town and Rural America in the '30's.

Washday at Stooksberry Homestead. Near Andersonville, Tennessee. October 23, 1933.

Mrs. Sarah J. Wilson. Bull's Gap, Tennessee. October 2, 1933.

148

Warehouse of Sandy Valley Wholesale Grocery. (Part of American Red Cross
program of disaster relief in the Drought of 1930-31.) Paintsville, Kentucky, 1931.

149

Pawnshop and Patron. Nashville, Tennessee. 1930 (?)

150   Typical Home of a Small Independent Farmer in the Kentucky Mountains.
Kentucky. 1931.

Grinding Cane for Sorghum at Stooksberry Homestead. Near Andersonville, Tennessee. October 23, 1933.

Watermill Grinding Meal, run by H. L. Nicely, son of J. C. Nicely. Goin, Tennessee. November 8, 1933.

Store and Post Office at Goin, Tennessee. Mr. J. C. Nicely Has Been Storekeeper Here for 30 Years. November 8, 1933.

153

Interior View of Oakdale School. From 30-40 Pupils Usually Attend.
Near Layston, Tennessee. October 23, 1933.

Another of the Children of War Veterans Living in Foothills of Ozarks,
Who Lost All of His Foodstuffs in the Drought. Near Damascus, Arkansas. 1931.

156

Colored Beneficiary of the Red Cross in Ozark Foothills. Near Damascus, Arkansas. 1931.